Reading Grade 1

Best Value Books

Table Of Contents

The student pages in this book have been specially prepared for reproduction on any standard copying machine.

Kelley Wingate products are available at fine educational supply stores throughout the U. S. and Canada.

First Grade Skills **CD-3708** Printed in the United States Of America ISBN 0-88724-426-2

Estimating Reading Ability

The following graded word lists may be used to estimate a student's reading grade level.

1. Ask the student to read each word in the list.

2. Keep count of the number of words the student reads from the list.

3. Estimate the student's ability to read materials at the same grade level as the grade level of the word list. Base your estimate upon:

23 or more The student can probably read at this grade level without help.

18 - 22 The student can probably read at this grade level if given some help.

17 or less The student can probably not read at this grade level even if given help.

1. apple
2. begin
3. bone
4. class
5 country
6. drink
7. far
8. gave
9. ground
10. hold
11. keep
12. line
13. mix
14. never
15. pan
16. quiet
17. secret
18. sorry
19. store
20. these
21. track
22. watch
23. without
24. zoo
25. smell

Ready-To-Use Ideas and Activities

The activities in this book will help children master the basic skills necessary to become competent learners. Remember as you read through the activities listed below, as you go through this book, that all children learn at their own rate. Although repetition is important, it is critical that we never lose sight of the fact that it is equally important to build children's self-esteem and self-confidence if we want them to become successful learners as well as good citizens.

Story Comprehension
During or after story discussion, there are two different types of questions that you can ask to ensure and enhance reading comprehension. The first type of question is a factual question. This type of question includes question words such as: who, what, when, where, and why. It can also include questions like How old is the character?, Where does the character live?, What time was it when....?, or any question that has a clear answer. The other type of question is an open-ended question. These questions will not have a clear answer. They are based on opinions about the story, not on facts. An open-ended question can be something like: Why do you think the character acted as he did?, How do you think the character felt about her actions or the actions of others?, What do you think the character will do next?, or What other ways could this story have ended?.

The back of this book has removable flash cards that will be great for use for basic skill and enrichment activities. Pull the flash cards out and either cut them apart or, if you have access to a paper cutter, use that to cut the flash cards apart. The following is just one of the ways you may want to use these flash cards.

Reproduce the bingo sheet on the opposite page in this book, making enough to have one for each student. Hand them out to the students. Take the flashcards and write the words on the chalk board. Have the students choose 24 of the words and write them in any order on the empty spaces of their bingo cards, writing only one word in each space. When all students have finished their cards, take the flashcards and make them in to a deck. Call out the words one at a time. Any student who has a word that you call out should make an "X" through the word to cross it out. The student who crosses out five words in a row first (Horizontally, vertically, or diagonally) wins the game. To extend the game you can continue playing until you a student crosses out all of the words on his bingo sheet.

Vocabulary Bingo

		FREE		

Name ________________________________ skill: beginning reading- completing sentences

Read the sentences. Fill in the blanks.

My name is Bob.

I am six years old.

1. ____________ name is Bob.

2. My ____________ is Bob.

3. My name is ____________.

4. ____________ am six years old.

5. I am ____________ years old.

6. My ____________ is ____________.

7. ____________ am ____________ years old.

Name ________________________________

skill: beginning reading-
completing sentences

Read the sentences. Fill in the blanks.

Meg

This girl is Meg.
She is my sister.

1. ______ girl is Meg.

2. This ______ is Meg.

3. This girl is ______.

4. ______ is my sister.

5. She is ______ sister.

6. This ______ is ______ .

7. ______ is ______ sister.

Name ________________________________

skill: beginning reading-
completing sentences

Read the sentences. Fill in the blanks.

School

We go to school.
We ride the bus.

1. __________ go to school.

2. We __________ to school.

3. We go to __________ .

4. We __________ the bus.

5. We ride the __________ .

6. We __________ to __________ .

7. __________ ride __________ bus.

Name ____________________

skill: beginning reading-
completing sentences

Read the sentences. Fill in the blanks.

Run and Play

Bob can run fast.
Meg likes to play ball.

1. Bob ________ run fast.

2. Bob can ________ fast.

3. Bob can run ________ .

4. Meg ________ to play ball.

5. Meg likes to ________ ball.

6. Bob ________ run ________ .

7. Meg ________ to ________ ball.

Name ______________________________ skill: beginning reading- completing sentences

Read the sentences. Fill in the blanks.

Miss Snow

Miss Snow works at school.
She helps Meg and Bob read.

1. Miss ______ works at school.

2. Miss Snow ______ at school.

3. Miss Snow works ______ school.

4. She ______ Meg and Bob read.

5 She helps Meg and Bob ______.

6. ______ Snow ______ at school.

7. ______ helps ______ and Bob read.

Name ____________________

skill: beginning reading-
completing sentences

Read the sentences. Fill in the blanks.

Bill

Our class has a pet.
His name is Bill.

1. ________ class has a pet.

2. Our ________ has a pet.

3. Our class has a ________ .

4. ________ name is Bill.

5. His name is ________ .

6. ________ class ________ a pet.

7. His ________ is ________ .

Name ______________________________

skill: beginning reading-
completing sentences

Read the sentences. Fill in the blanks.

A Fish

This fish is funny.
It is blue and yellow.

1. This ____________ is funny.
2. This fish is ____________ .
3. ____________ is blue and yellow.
4. It is ____________ and yellow.
5. It is blue and ____________ .
6. This ____________ is ____________ .
7. It is ____________ and ____________ .

Name ____________________________________

skill: beginning reading-
completing sentences

Read the sentences. Fill in the blanks.

Ready To Go

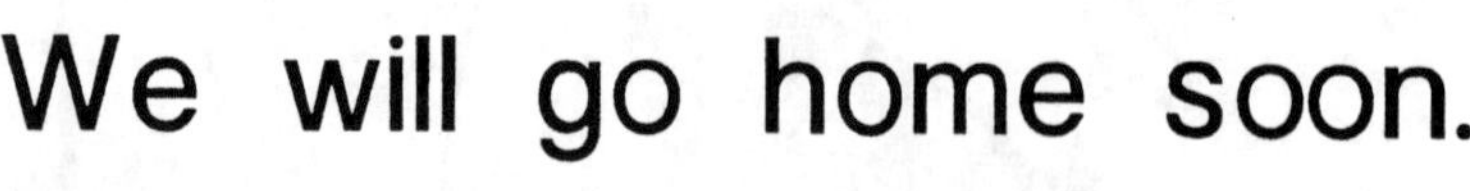

We will go home soon.

Get ready to go!

1. We ____________ go home soon.

2. We will go ____________ soon.

3. We will go home ____________ .

4. We ____________ go ____________ soon.

5. ____________ ready to go.

6. Get ____________ to go.

7. Get ____________ to ____________ !

Name ____________________

skill: beginning reading-
completing sentences

Read the sentences. Fill in the blanks.

Mother

Mother is at the bus stop.
She walks us home.

1. ______ is at the bus stop.
2. Mother is ______ the bus stop.
3. Mother is at the bus ______.
4. ______ walks us home.
5. She ______ us home.
6. She walks us ______.
7. ______ walks us ______.

Name ____________________

skill: beginning reading-completing sentences

Read the sentences. Fill in the blanks.

Good Cookies

We will eat something now.
Cookies and milk are good!

1. We will ________ something now.
2. We will eat something ________ .
3. ________ and milk are good!
4. Cookies and ________ are good!
5. Cookies and milk are ________ !
6. We ________ eat something ________ .
7. ________ and ________ are good!

Name ________________________________

skill: beginning reading-
answering questions

Read the story and answer the questions.

Jim

Jim is Bob's friend.
They play with trains and trucks.
They make up games with these toys.

1. Who is Jim?
____

2. Who is Bob's friend?
____

3. Who plays with trains and trucks?
____

4. What toys do Jim and Bob play with?
____

5. Are apples and cookies toys?
____

Name ____________________

skill: beginning reading-answering questions

Read the story and answer the questions.

Peg

Peg comes to play with Meg.
She has a big blue bike.
Meg has some green skates and a doll.

1. Who comes to play with Meg?

2. What does Peg's bike look like?

3. What color are the skates?

4. Who has the doll?

5. What two toys does Meg have?

Name ______________________________

skill: beginning reading-
answering questions

Read the story and answer the questions.

The Race

Peg had a race with Jim.
They ran from the tree to the sidewalk.
Peg fell down and Jim won the race.

1. Who had a race?

____

2. Where did they run?

____

3. Who fell down?

____

4. Who won the race?

____

5. Why did Peg lose the race?

____

Name ______________________________

skill: beginning reading-
answering questions

Read the story and answer the questions.

A Party

The children had a party.
The boys blew up balloons.
The girls gave cake to everyone.
They laughed and had fun.

1. What did the children have?

____

2. Who had the party?

____

3. Who blew up the balloons?

____

4. What did the girls do?

____

5. What did they do at the party?

____

Name ______________________________

skill: beginning reading-
answering questions

Read the story and answer the questions.

The Surprise

Meg and Peg hid behind the tree.
Bob and Jim were walking across the yard.
The girls jumped out from behind the tree.
The boys were very surprised!

1. Where did the girls hide?

2. Who was walking across the yard?

3. What did the girls do first?

4. Who was surprised?

5. How did the girls surprise the boys?

Name ________________________________

skill: beginning reading-
answering questions

Read the story and answer the questions.

Train

Bob was playing with his train.
The train fell off the table.
A wheel was broken.
Father helped Bob put it back on the train.

1. What was Bob playing with?

2. Whose train was it?

3. What happened to the train?

4. What was broken?

5. Who helped Bob?

skill: beginning reading-
answering questions

Name ______________________________

Read the story and answer the questions.

The Book

Meg was reading a big brown book.

The book was about a little girl and her cat.

The girl was named Evie.

The cat was named Socks because he had black feet.

Meg liked the story very much.

1. What color was the book?

2. What was the story about?

3. Who was Evie?

4. Why was the cat named Socks?

5. Was Socks a boy or a girl?

6. Did Meg like the book?

Name ____________________

skill: beginning reading-
answering questions

Read the story and answer the questions.

School Play

One day there was a funny play at school.

Bob and Jim were clowns.

Peg and Meg were lions.

All the mothers and fathers came to see it.

They laughed and clapped when it was over.

1. What did the mothers and fathers come to see?

2. Who were clowns?

3. What were Peg and Meg?

4. Where was the play?

5. Did the mothers and fathers like the play?

6. What did they do when it was over?

Name ______________________

skill: beginning reading- answering questions

Read the story and answer the questions.

On the Farm

Mother and Father took Meg and Bob to a farm.

There were many baby animals to pet.

Meg fed a little white goat.

Bob rode a tall brown horse.

The wagon ride was the most fun of all.

1. Where did Meg and Bob go?

2. What did they pet?

3. Who fed the goat?

4. What was the most fun of all?

5. What did the goat look like?

6. What did Bob ride on?

Name________________________________

skill: beginning reading-
answering questions

Read the story and answer the questions.

Fishing

It was a warm and sunny day.
Bob and Jim went fishing at the pond.
Jim caught a green fish and a yellow fish.
Bob caught a large black fish.
The boys let their fish go.
They wanted to catch the fish again some other day.

1. Where did Bob and Jim go?

2. Who caught the large black fish?

3. What did the boys do with their fish?

4. What did Jim catch?

5. What kind of day was it?

6. Why did they let the fish go?

7. Who caught the most fish?

Name____ skill: beginning reading-answering questions

Read the story and answer the questions.

Matt the Bat

Matt is a bat. He has many pals to play with. They all go to school. It is a bat school. He learns to fly. He likes to read books, too!

1. What is Matt?

____

2. What does Matt do with his pals?

____

3. Where do they go?

____

4. What school do they go to?

____

5. What does Matt do at school?

____

6. What does Matt like to do?

____

7. Is this story real or make-believe?

____

Name____

skill: beginning reading-
answering questions

Read the story and answer the questions.

The Little Egg

Mother Hen had one little egg. She sat on it for many days. The other hens said her egg was too little. It was not a good egg. Mother Hen did not listen. One day the little egg opened. Out came the biggest chick of all!

1. What did Mother Hen have?

____

2. How long did she sit on it?

____

3. What did the other hens say?

____

4. Was the egg good?

____

5. Did Mother Hen listen to the others?

____

6. What came out of the little egg?

____

7. Can hens talk?

____

Name ______________________________

skill: beginning reading-answering questions

Read the story and answer the questions.

Ben

Ben the puppy wanted to play. No one was home. Jim was at school. Ben looked in his box. There was a ball. There was a sock. But there was no one to play with. Ben was sad. The door opened. Jim was home!

1. Who was Ben?

____

2. What did he want to do?

____

3. Who was home?

____

4. Where was Jim?

____

5. What was in Ben's box?

____

6. How did Ben feel?

____

7. How did Ben feel when Jim came home?

____

Name ________________________________

skill: beginning reading-
answering questions

Read the story and answer the questions.

Sue

Sue is a skunk. She likes children. She wants to play with them. Children run away from her. They are afraid. This makes Sue very sad, but she has a plan. Today Sue will go to the zoo. She will ask if she can stay there. Do you think Sue can stay?

1. Who is Sue?

   ____

2. What does Sue like to do?

   ____

3. What do children do when they see Sue?

   ____

4. Why do they run away?

   ____

5. Where will Sue go?

   ____

6. What will Sue ask at the zoo?

   ____

7. Is this story real or make-believe?

   ____

Name ______________________________

skill: beginning reading-
answering questions

Read the story and answer the questions.

Lenny

Lenny was a big cat. One day a man took him away. He put Lenny in the circus. Why put a cat in the circus? Lenny did not know. Each day Lenny grew bigger. He learned new tricks. One day Lenny tried to meow. Out came a big roar. "What a good joke," said Lenny. "I am really a lion!"

1. What did Lenny think he was?

____

2. Where did the man take Lenny?

____

3. What did Lenny do each day?

____

4. What did Lenny learn?

____

5. What happened when he tried to meow?

____

6. What was Lenny really?

____

7. Is this story real or make-believe?

____

Name ____________________

skill: beginning reading-answering questions

Finding Food

Boo was a bear cub. Every morning he went with his mother to find food. He was not much help to Mother. He liked to play with the flowers and other baby animals. One day Boo saw a hole in a tree. He stuck in his paw. It was very sticky. Boo had found a honey hive!

1. What is the little bear's name?

____

2. What does he do every morning?

____

3. Why isn't Boo much help?

____

4. What did he see one day?

____

5. What did he do?

____

6. What had Boo found?

____

7. Draw a picture of Boo.

____

Name ____________________

skill: beginning reading-answering questions

Read the story and answer the questions.

Going to the Moon

We like to go to the moon. We go there every Saturday. The moon has lots of dust and rocks. I like to jump because I can go so high. My sister picks up rocks to bring home. We get back just in time for lunch.

1. Where do we like to go?

____

2. What day do we go there?

____

3. What is on the moon?

____

4. Who picks up rocks?

____

5. What do I like to do?

____

6. When do we get back?

____

7. Is this story real or make-believe?

____

Name____

skill: beginning reading-
answering questions

Read the story and answer the questions.

Randy

Randy was a red race car. He did not care about driving fast. He did not care about winning the race. He liked to go slow. He wanted to look at everything as he went. Randy never won a race, but he had a lot of fun.

1. What is the name of the race car?

____

2. What color is he?

____

3. How does he like to drive?

____

4. Did he care when he lost?

____

5. What does Randy like to do when he drives?

____

6. How many races has Randy won?

____

7. Is this story real or make-believe?

____

Name____

skill: beginning reading-
answering questions

Read the story and answer the questions.

Under the Sea

If I could live anywhere it would be under the sea. I would live in a glass house so I could watch the fish. I would grow seaweed to eat. I would ride seahorses to school. The fish would be my best friends. You could come to see me. You would get wet!

1. Where would I like to live?

   ____

2. What would my house be made of?

   ____

3. What food would I eat?

   ____

4. How would I get to school?

   ____

5. Who would be my friends?

   ____

6. Is this story real or make-believe?

   ____

7. Draw a picture of my sea house.

   ____

Name ______________________________

skill: beginning reading-answering questions

Read the story and answer the questions.

Jill the Giant

Jill was a giant. She was the only giant in Little Town. Poor Jill. The children were afraid of her. She was too big. One day she saw a boy named John in a tree. He could not get down. Jill helped John. She took him from the tree and put him on the ground. Then the children liked her.

1. What was Jill?

   ____

2. Why were the children afraid of her?

   ____

3. Who was in the tree?

   ____

4. What was wrong with John?

   ____

5. What did Jill do?

   ____

6. How did the children feel after that?

   ____

7. Is this story real or make-believe?

   ____

Name______________________________________

Read the story and answer the questions.

Bats

There is a bat in this cave. He is sleeping. He holds on with his feet. Bats sleep all day. They fly out of the cave at night. They eat bugs that fly.

1. What is in the cave?

____

2. What is the bat doing?

____

3. How does he hold on?

____

4. When do bats go out of the cave?

____

5. What do bats eat?

____

6. Name another animal that sleeps all day.

____

Name____

skill: beginning reading-
answering questions

Read the story and answer the questions.

Chicken Eggs

Chickens are birds. The hens lay eggs. They sit on the eggs to warm them. The baby chicks grow inside the eggs. When the chick is ready it pecks at the shell. Out pops a new chick!

1. What are chickens?

   ____

2. Who lays the eggs?

   ____

3. How do they keep the eggs warm?

   ____

4. What grows inside the egg?

   ____

5. When does the chick come out?

   ____

6. Name another animal that lays eggs.

   ____

Name____________________________________

skill: beginning reading-
answering questions

Read the story and answer the questions.

The Zoo

Many wild animals live at the zoo. Brown bears eat fish. Lions sleep in the sun. Seals splash playfully in the water. Most children like the monkeys best. The zoo is fun!

1. Where do many wild animals live?

____

2. What does the bear eat?

____

3. Which animals do most children like best?

____

4. What do the seals like to do?

____

5. Who sleeps in the sun?

____

6. Name another animal you can see at the zoo.

____

Name________________________________ skill: beginning reading-answering questions

Read the story and answer the questions.

The Circus

The circus is not like a zoo. Circus animals can do tricks. Bears dance and ride bikes. Tigers jump through hoops. People also do tricks. Some swing high in the air. The clowns make everyone laugh. It is a good show!

1. What is this story about?

   ____

2. What animal rides a bike?

   ____

3. Where do tigers jump?

   ____

4. What do the bears do?

   ____

5. What tricks can people do?

   ____

6. Draw a picture of the third sentence.

   ____

Name____

skill: beginning reading-
answering questions

Read the story an[illegible] r the questions.

[illegible] od Star

The sun is a star. [illegible] from where we live. The sun looks like a big ball. It is very hot. We need the sun's light. It keeps us warm. It helps plants grow. The sun is a good star for us.

1. What is this story about?

____

2. What is the sun?

____

3. What does the sun look like?

____

4. What does the sun feel like?

____

5. How does the sun help us?

____

6. How does the sun help plants?

____

Name____________________________________ skill: beginning reading-answering questions

Read the story and answer the questions.

Trees

Trees are the biggest plant of all. They have roots in the dirt. The roots take in water. Trees have leaves. The leaves use sunlight to make food. We sit in the shade under trees. We use the wood to make many things.

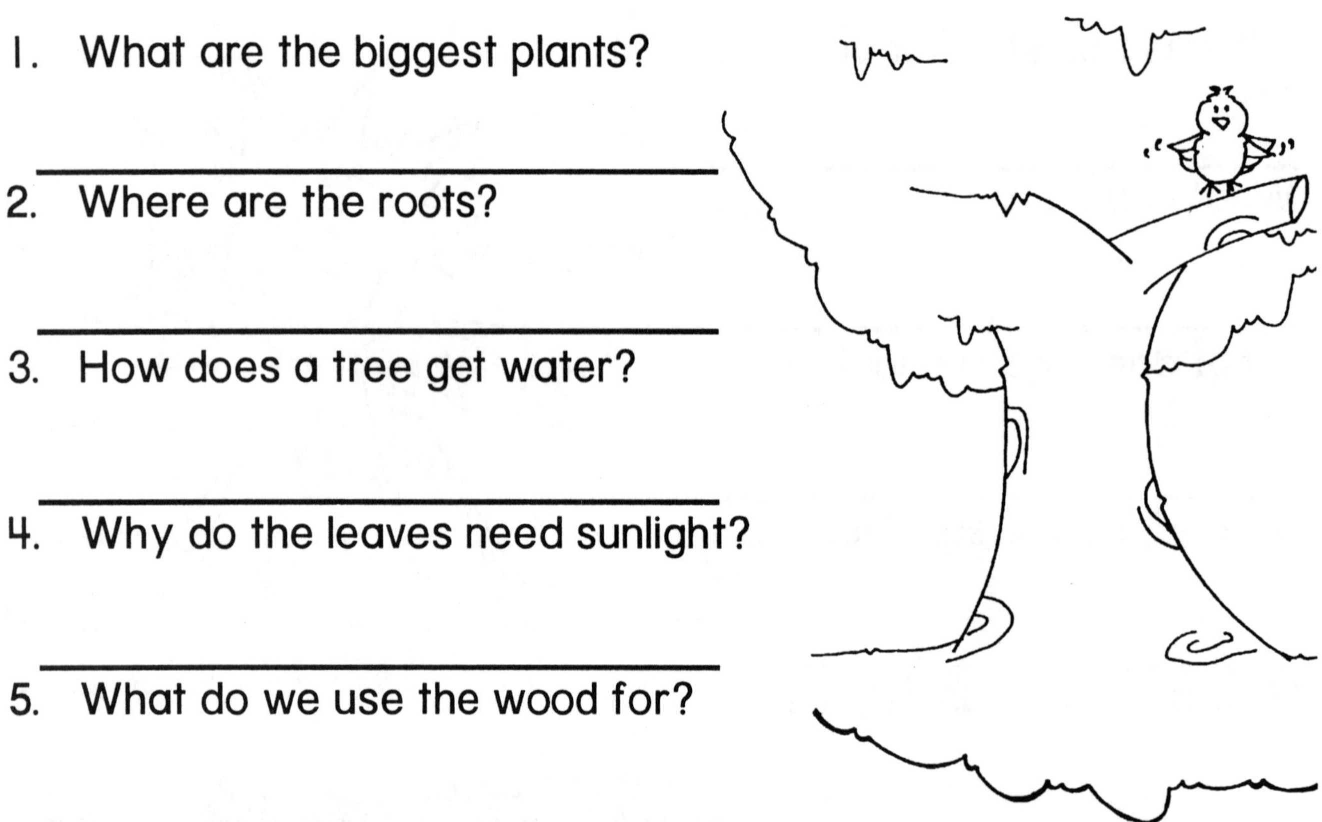

1. What are the biggest plants?

____

2. Where are the roots?

____

3. How does a tree get water?

____

4. Why do the leaves need sunlight?

____

5. What do we use the wood for?

____

6. Draw a picture of yourself sitting in the shade of a tree.

____

Name________________________________

Read the story and answer the questions.

Ways to go

We have lots of ways to go places. We ride on bikes on sidewalks. Cars and buses drive on roads. Boats and ships sail on water. Airplanes and rockets fly in the air. Each trip can take us somewhere new.

1. What do we ride on sidewalks?

2. Where do boats and ships sail?

3. What do cars and buses do?

____

4. What can fly in the air?

____

5. What is this story about?

____

6. How did you get to school this morning?

____

Name________________________________

skill: beginning reading-
answering questions

Read the story and answer the questions.

Beavers

Beavers live in ponds. They have sharp teeth. They can cut down small trees. These trees are put into the pond to make a home. Beavers live with their families. Their flat tail helps them swim.

1. What is this story about?

____

2. Where do beavers live?

____

3. What do beavers make out of trees?

____

4. How do they cut the trees?

____

5. Who do beavers live with?

____

6. Why do beavers have flat tails?

____

Name ______________________________ skill: beginning reading-answering questions

Read the story and answer the questions.

Bears

Bears are big animals. They have fur to keep them warm. They have short tails. Bears can stand on their back feet. Then they are very tall! Most bears eat plants and bugs. In the fall they eat a lot. Then bears can sleep all winter.

1. What is this story about?

____

2. When are bears very tall?

____

3. Do bears have a long tail?

____

4. What do bears eat?

____

5. Why do bears eat a lot in the fall?

____

6. What keeps bears warm?

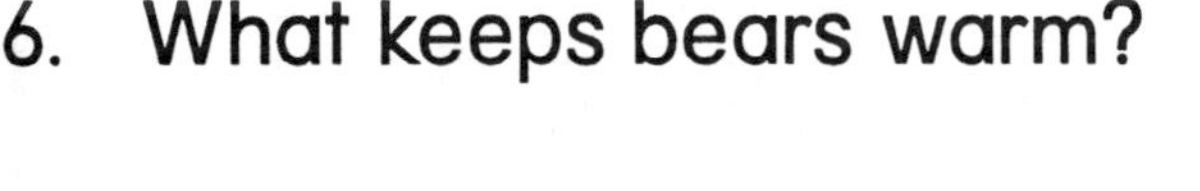

____

Name ____________________ skill: following directions

Read then do.

Here is a barn.
Color the barn red.
Draw three eggs near it.

Here is a book.
Write the word "read" on it.
Color the book blue.

Here is a cat.
Color the cat orange.
Draw a ball near the cat.

Here is a big truck.
Color the truck red.
Draw a blue ball on the truck.

Name ________________________________ skill: following directions

Read then do.

Here is a hen.

Color the hen brown.

Draw three eggs near it.

Here is a sock.

Color it black.

Draw another sock near it.

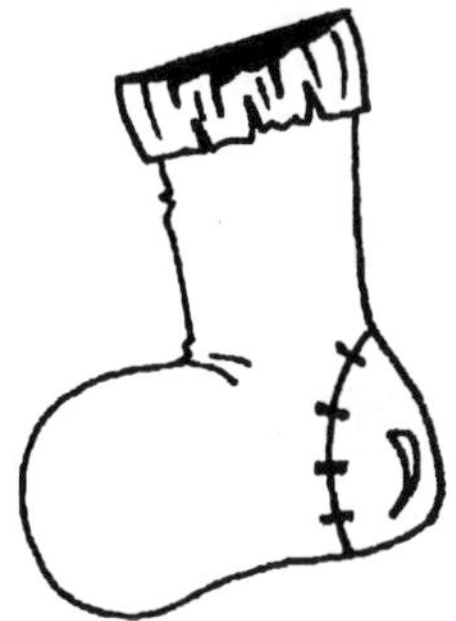

Here is a box.

Put a green ball in it.

Color the box orange.

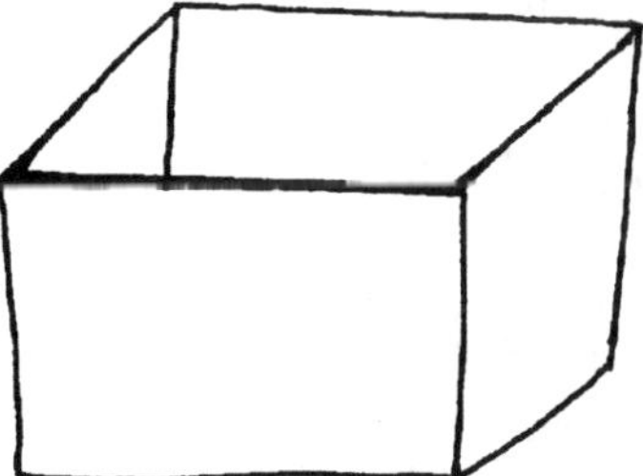

Here is a fish.

Color it yellow.

Draw three little fish near it.

Name________________________________ skill: following directions

Read then do.

Here are three books.

They are on the table.

Color two books green.

Draw an X on one book.

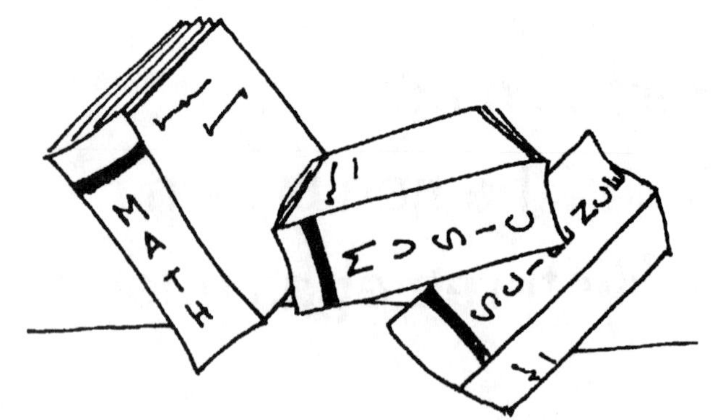

Bill is here.

His dog is here, too.

Color the dog.

Put a line under Bill.

Here is the school bus.

A girl is on the bus.

Put an X on the bus.

Circle one of the girls.

Here is a barn.

A cow is near the barn.

Put an X on the cow.

Put a line under the barn.

Name ________________________________ skill: following directions

Read then do.

Here is a glass of milk.

It is on the table.

Put a cookie near the glass.

Circle the glass of milk.

Here is a bed.

A cat is on the bed.

Put an X over the cat.

Circle the cat.

Here are three balls.

Color the biggest one green.

Put a line under the little one.

Put an X on the one with a star.

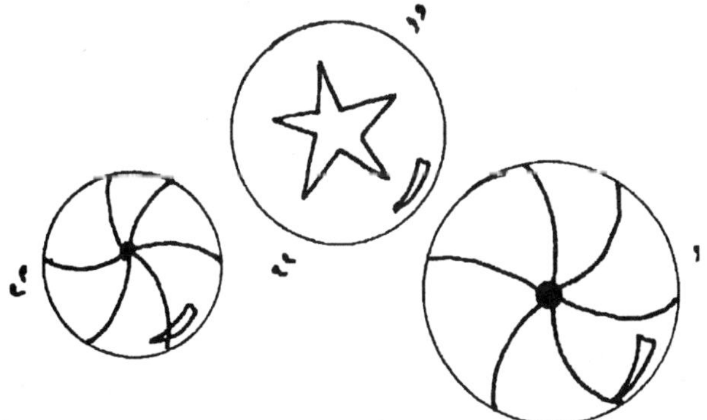

Here are three boxes.

Color the last one green.

Put an X on the first one.

Put a line under the big one.

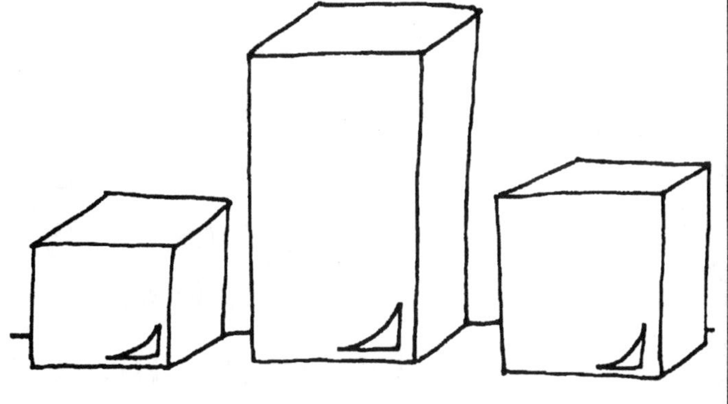

Name________________________________ skill: following directions

Read then draw a zoo.

Draw a big pool.
Put a seal near the pool.
Color the seal black or brown.
Draw a tree near the pool.
Draw a monkey near the tree.
Draw something for the monkey to eat.
Draw one more animal near the pool.

Name ______________________________ skill: following directions

Read then draw a farm.

Draw a big barn.
Color the barn red.
Draw two ducks near the barn.
Color the ducks white or yellow.
Put a cow in the barn.
Put a white and brown horse near the barn.
Put a girl on the horse.

Name________________________________ skill: sequencing

1. Read the story.

Baking a Cake

Meg is making a cake. She puts everything she needs into the bowl. Then she mixes the batter. The batter goes into the oven to bake. Soon it smells good.

2. Read the sentences below. Rewrite them in the correct order on the lines below.

Mix the batter.
The cake is baked.
Put everything in the bowl.
Put the batter in the oven.

1. ________________________________

2. ________________________________

3. ________________________________

4. ________________________________

Name____ skill: sequencing

1. Read the story.

Pet Fish

I have three pet fish. When I tap on the glass they swim to the top. I give them their food. I feed them until they are full. They wave their tails as they swim away.

2. Read the sentences below. Rewrite them in the correct order on the lines below.

They eat until they are full.
I tap on the glass.
I drop their food into the bowl.
They wave their tails.

1. ____

2. ____

3. ____

4. ____

Name ______________________________ skill: sequencing

1. Read the story.

Ready for School

It is time for school. I ate my eggs and toast. I drank my juice. I washed my face then brushed my teeth. I got dressed before the bus came.

2. Read the sentences below. Rewrite them in the correct order on the lines below.

Get dressed.
Eat breakfast.
Brush your teeth.
Wash your face.

1. ______________________________

2. ______________________________

3. ______________________________

4. ______________________________

Name______________________________ skill: sequencing

1. Read the story.

Making Lunch

Sue will fix her own lunch. First, she will open the can of soup. Then she heats the soup on the stove. It tastes good. Last, Sue cleans the dishes.

2. Read the sentences below. Rewrite them in the correct order on the lines below.

Open up the soup.
Clean up the dishes.
Eat the soup.
Heat up the soup.

1. ______________________________

2. ______________________________

3. ______________________________

4. ______________________________

Name________________________________ skill: sequencing

I. Read the story.

Plant a Seed

We planted some apple seeds. We watered them every day. They grew into small plants. Now they are small trees. Someday we will eat the apples that grow on them.

2. Read the sentences below. Rewrite them in the correct order on the lines below.

We watered the seeds.
We have small apple trees.
We planted some apple seeds.
Small plants grew from the seeds.

I. ________________________________

2. ________________________________

3. ________________________________

4. ________________________________

Name______________________________ skill: sequencing

1. Read the story.

New Clothes

Ted needed some new clothes. He needed socks, shoes, and shirts. He made a list of what he needed to buy. Mother drove him to the store. They found all the things on his list then paid for them.

2. Read the sentences below. Rewrite them in the correct order on the lines below.

Ted made a list of what he needed.
Mother took him to the store.
Ted paid for the new clothes.
They found everything on the list.

1. ______________________________

2. ______________________________

3. ______________________________

4. ______________________________

Name____________________________________ skill: sequencing

1. Read the story.

Soccer

Today was my first soccer lesson. The teacher said, "My name is Beth. I will be your teacher. Please sit down on the grass." We learned how to kick the ball. It was fun.

2. Read the sentences below. Rewrite them in the correct order on the lines below.

"My name is Beth."

I learned to kick the ball.

"Please sit down."

Today I had a soccer lesson.

1. ____________________________________

2. ____________________________________

3. ____________________________________

4. ____________________________________

Name____ skill: sequencing

1. Read the story.

The Letter

Ann got a new bike for her birthday. Grandpa gave it to her. Ann wrote a thank-you letter. She mailed the letter. After he opened the letter, Grandpa read it. He was very happy.

2. Read the sentences below. Rewrite them in the correct order on the lines below.

Ann wrote a letter.

Grandpa opened the letter.

Ann got a new bike.

Ann mailed the letter.

Grandpa was happy.

1. ____

2. ____

3. ____

4. ____

5. ____

Name ____________________ skill: sequencing

1. Read the story.

Swimming

I have on my swimsuit. Let's go to your house to play. We can run in the sprinkler. Then we can swim in the pool. We will dry off on the big brown towels and then have lunch.

2. Read the sentences below. Rewrite them in the correct order on the lines below.

We can have lunch.

We can get wet in the sprinkler.

We will use towels to dry off.

We will go to your house.

We will go in the pool.

1. ____________________

2. ____________________

3. ____________________

4. ____________________

5. ____________________

Name ____________________ skill: sequencing

1. Read the story.

Make a Kite

Today we made a kite. Susan had the sticks. Peter cut the paper to fit. Jack pasted it together. I put on the string and then the tail. Let's go fly a kite.

2. Read the sentences below. Rewrite them in the correct order on the lines below.

Fly the kite.

Lay the paper on the sticks.

Put on string and a tail.

We want to make a kite.

Paste the paper on the sticks.

1. ____________________

2. ____________________

3. ____________________

4. ____________________

5. ____________________

Name________________________________ skill: sequencing

1. Read the story.

Ready to go

"We must hurry, " said Mother. " We are almost late." I put on my socks. Mother tied my shoes. We brushed my hair then put a ribbon in it. Mother started the car. Now we are ready.

2. Read the sentences below. Rewrite them in the correct order on the lines below.

I put my socks and shoes on.

Mother put a ribbon in my hair.

My hair was brushed.

We are ready to go.

Mother started the car.

1. ______________________________

2. ______________________________

3. ______________________________

4. ______________________________

5. ______________________________

Name________________________________ skill: sequencing

1. Read the story.

Go to Bed

Every night Max gets ready for bed. First he takes a bath in the tub. Next he gets out the toothbrush and paste. He brushes up and down very well. Then Father reads a good-night story to him. Last, Max closes his eyes to sleep.

2. Read the sentences below. Rewrite them in the correct order on the lines below.

Father reads a story.

Max brushes his teeth.

Max closes his eyes.

He gets out the toothbrush.

Max takes a bath.

1. ________________________________

2. ________________________________

3. ________________________________

4. ________________________________

5. ________________________________

Name ______________________ skill: sequencing

1. Read the story.

The Snake

There is a little snake in my yard. He lives under the rose bush. He eats flies and other bugs. My mother does not mind having him there. She says he is helpful. I call the snake Stripes. He is kind of like a pet to me.

2. Read the sentences below. Rewrite them in the correct order on the lines below.

He lives under a bush.

Mother says he is helpful.

We have a snake in our yard.

He is like a pet.

The snake eats flies and bugs.

1. ______________________

2. ______________________

3. ______________________

4. ______________________

5. ______________________

Name____ skill: sequencing

1. Read the story.

Pizza

Pizza is my favorite food. Mother calls the store and tells them what we want. Soon someone brings it to our door. It smells so good! Father cuts the pieces and puts them on a plate. I can eat three or four pieces because I really like it.

2. Read the sentences below. Rewrite them in the correct order on the lines below.

Someone brings it to our door.
I eat many pieces.
Father cuts the pizza.
Mother calls to order the pizza.
He puts the pieces on our plates.

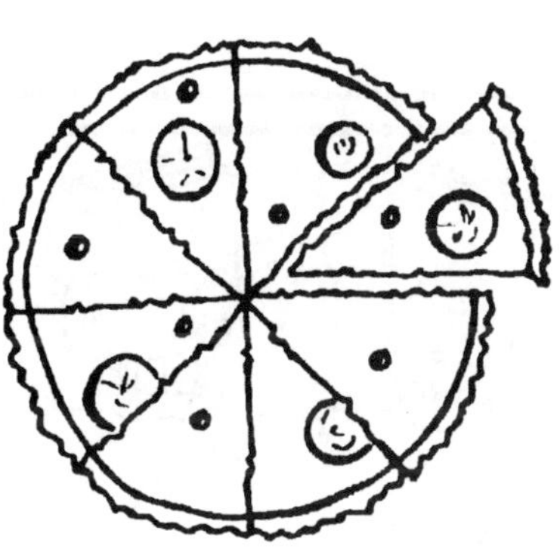

1. ____

2. ____

3. ____

4. ____

5. ____

Name______________________________ skill: inflections/"s" endings

In each row choose the correct description for each picture and write it in the blank.

one kitten

two kittens

three kittens

______________ ______________

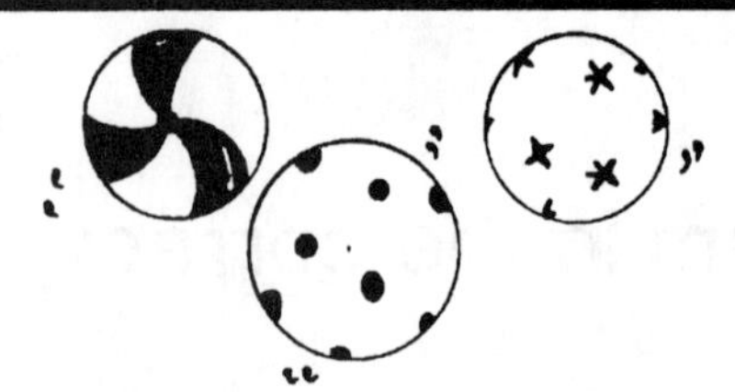

one ball

two balls

three balls

______________ ______________

one book

two books

three books

______________ ______________

one boy

two boys

three boys

______________ ______________

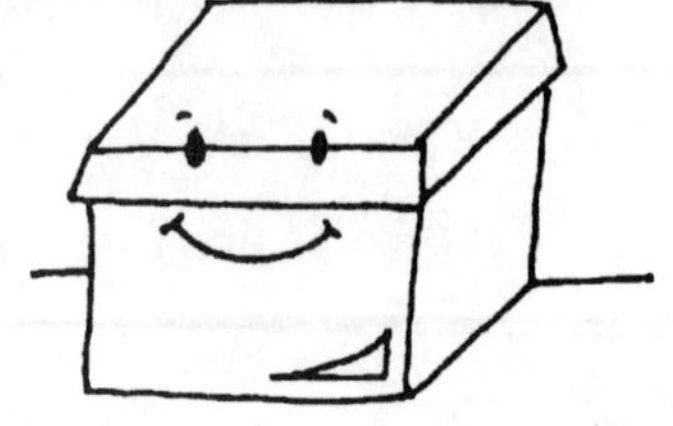

one box

two boxes

three boxes

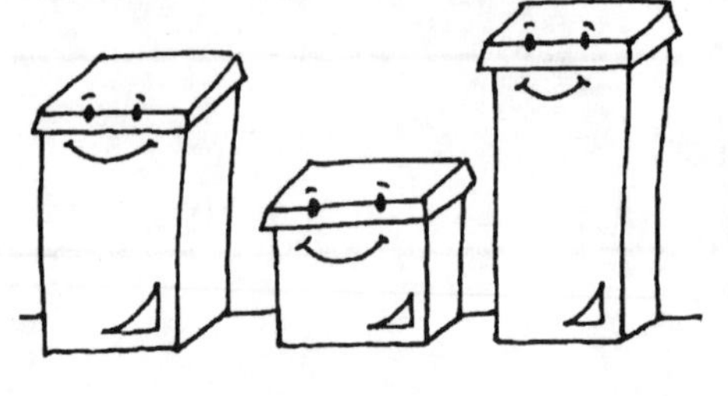

______________ ______________

Name ______________________ skill: "s" endings

1. [illegible] cle the word that best describes

house		houses
dog		dogs
girl		girls
tree		trees

2. Draw a little red house with two green trees near it.

Name________________________________ skill: inflections/"s" endings

Choose the correct word for each sentence.

1. I can ________ to the party. Jim ________ to my house. come comes	2. Peg ________ to be alone. We ________ a cookie. want wants
3. She will ________ it to me. He ________ me one. give gives	4. Meg can ________ the play. She ________ a dog. see sees
5. Who ________ fast? We ________ fast? run runs	6. I ________ at a joke. She ________ a lot. laugh laughs
7. Bob ________ high. Jim can ________ higher. jump jumps	8. I ________ on one foot. She ________ over a ball. hop hops

Name________________________________ skill: inflections/"s" endings

Circle the correct word in each box.

bird birds	snake snakes	eye eyes
flower flowers	chair chairs	window windows
kite kites	coat coats	bat bats
hole holes	pot pots	train trains

Name ____________________ skill: inflections/"es" endings

Choose the correct word for each sentence.

1. I have a ______ . There are two ______ . box boxes	2. The ______ is red. Three ______ are red. fox foxes
3. I made two ______ today. I made a ______ on a star. wish wishes	4. ______ are fun to make! What is for ______ ? lunch lunches
5. ______ your hands. Beth ______ the dishes. wash washes	6. That ______ me up! Please ______ the cards. mix mixes
7. Father ______ the tire. I can help ______ it. fix fixes	8. Will you ______ the play. Bob ______ with us. watch watches

Name________________________________ skill: inflections/"er" endings

Fill in the blank with the correct word.

1. The dog is________than the cat.	big	bigger
2. The bird is________than the house.	high	higher
3. It is a________day.	hot	hotter
4. The bear is very________.	fat	fatter
5. I have a________ puppy.	small	smaller
6. He is a ________boy.	tall	taller
7. Her dress is________than yours.	long	longer
8. I am a ________runner.	fast	faster
9. The turtle is________than the rabbit.	slower	slow
10. That was a________story.	short	shorter

Name____________________________________ skill: inflections/"ed" endings

Fill in the blank with the correct word.

1. Jim ________ for the ball.	look	looked
2. Meg can ________ high.	jump	jumped
3. Bob ________ his father.	help	helped
4. We ________ to go now.	want	wanted
5. Peg likes to ________ at school.	work	worked
6. I will ________ tonight.	play	played
7. Mother ________ my picture.	like	liked
8. The funny play made us ________.	laugh	laughed
9. Mother ________ the dish.	wash	washed
10. Peg will ________ to the store.	walk	walked

Name ______________________________ skill: inflections/ "er" or "ed"

Fill in the blank with the correct word.

1. Meg ________ at Peg and Jim.	smile	smiled
2. They were ________ home.	near	neared
3. It was ________ than before.	dark	darker
4. They saw a ________ bat!	brown	browner
5. Meg ________ the light to Jim.	hand	handed
6. Bill ________ across the grass.	hop	hopped
7. He ________ to eat grass.	love	loved
8. Peg will take ________ of Bill.	care	cared
9. Meg will ________ Peg how.	show	showed
10. They had a ________ time!	great	greater

Name________________________________ skill: inflections/"ed" endings

Fill in the blank with the correct word.

1. The cake is ________ .	bake	baked
2. The children will________ now.	start	started
3. We have________to a new house.	move	moved
4. His________is Bill.	name	named
5. I will take a ________soon.	trip	tripped
6. Peg is a good________ .	dance	dancer
7. Jim can________the others.	trick	tricked
8. Meg is a________in class!	talk	talker
9. Mr. Brown can________cakes.	bake	baker
10. Bob is ________than Jim.	fast	faster

Name________________________________

skill: recognizing beginning consonants

In each box draw a line to match the letter to the picture that begins with that letter.

l f p b	h d m r
m d c l	n g w y
p t b s	b k m j

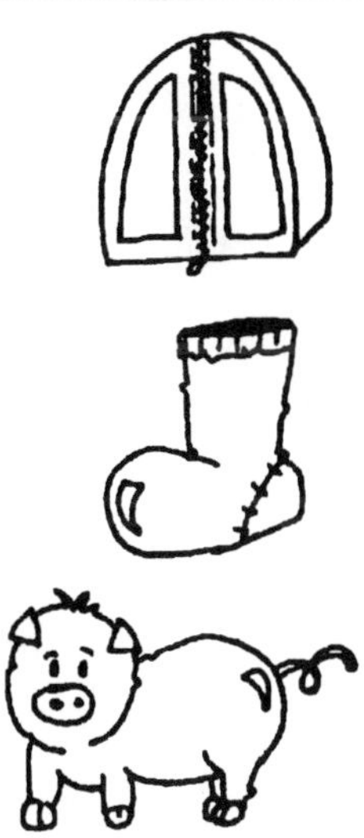

MATH

Name___________________________________

skill: recognizing beginning consonants

In each box draw a line to match the letter to the picture that begins with that letter.

N C Y S	Z T M K
S T C B	P F V H
W M D G	L D P R

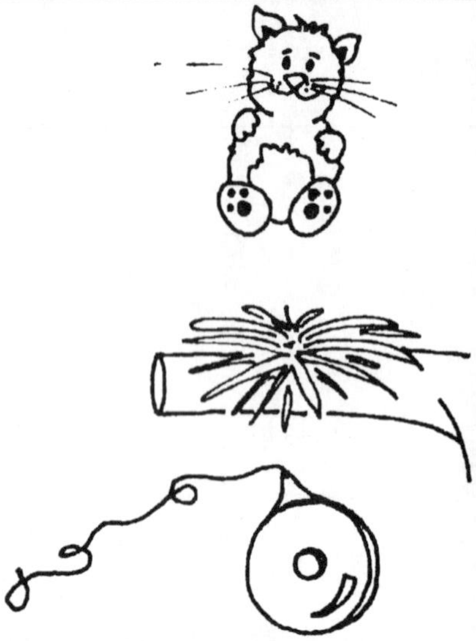

Name______________________________________ skill: recognizing beginning consonants

In each box circle the picture that begins with the same letter as the letter at the top of the box.

B b	T t	H h
S s	W w	G g
R r	L l	P p

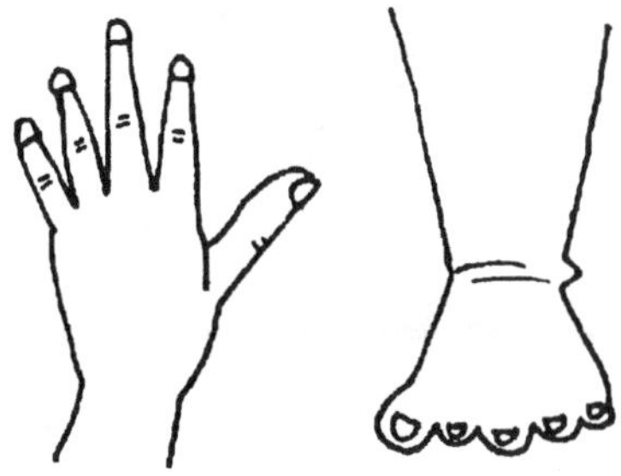

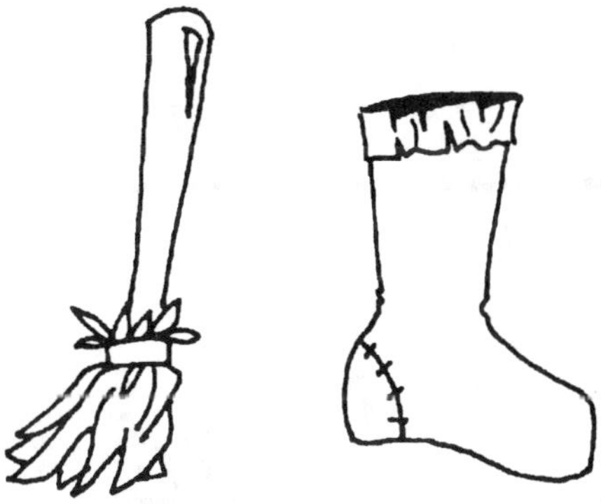

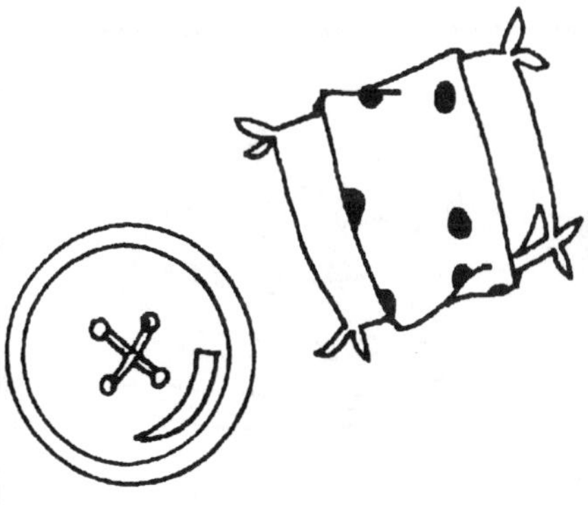

Name______________________________________

skill: recognizing beginning consonants

In each box circle the letter that the picture begins with.

Name_______________________________________ skill: recognizing ending consonants

In each box draw a line to match the letter to the picture that ends with the same letter.

r n t p	p g d l
t s l f	t m k n
d l t b	g m s r

Name________________________________

skill: recognizing ending consonants

In each box draw a line to match the letter to the picture that ends with the same letter.

M T F S	D L N G
N S F P	N D R G
M F G K	L T D R

Name ______________________________

skill: recognizing ending consonants

In each box draw a line to match the letter to the picture that ends with the same letter.

R r	D d	P p
N n	K k	M m
S s	L l	T t

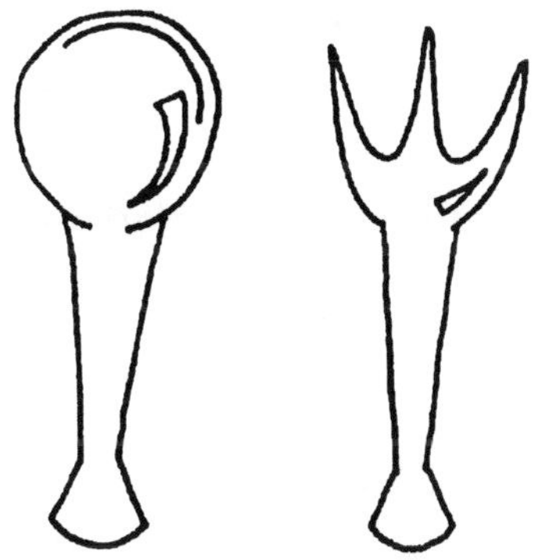

MATH BOOK

GUM

Name________________________________

skill: recognizing ending consonants

In each box draw a line to match the letter to the picture that ends with the same letter.

 p l b	 s m t	 b d s
 k r t	 n p h	 l r g
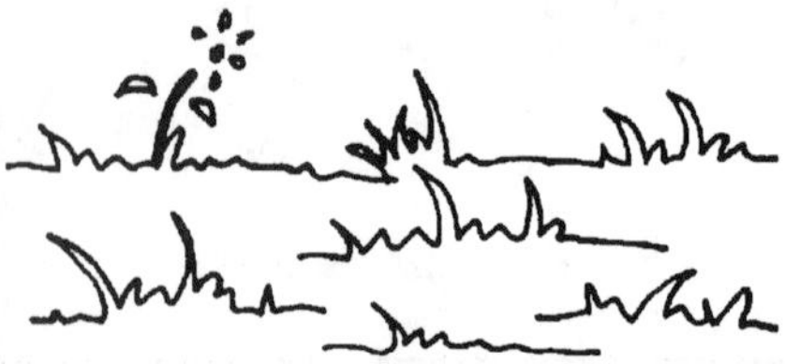 M S X	 B L N	 P M K
 T D R	 S N L	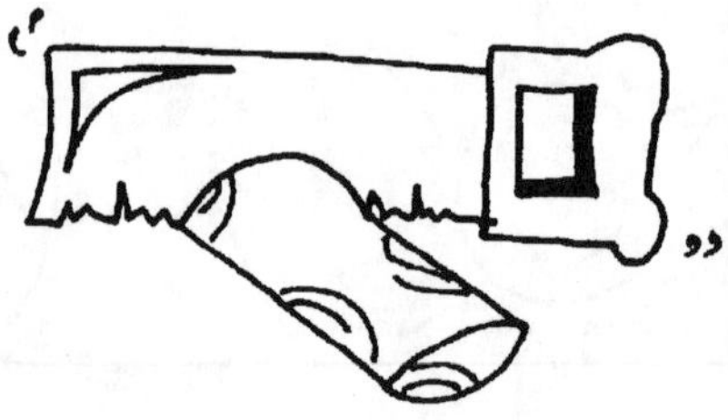 B W H

skill: recognizing beginning and ending consonants

Name ______________________________

In each box fill in the blanks to complete the word.

Name________________________________

skill: recognizing beginning and ending consonants

In each box fill in the blanks to complete the word.

Name ______________________________ skill: categorizing

In each row circle the word that is the opposite of the first word.

1. boy	boat	go	girl
2. hot	cold	see	hat
3. up	barn	down	on
4. sun	now	was	moon
5. on	ball	top	off
6. stop	hop	go	dog
7. went	came	her	sent
8. hello	yellow	sun	good-by

Name____ skill: categorizing

In each row circle the word that is the opposite of the first word.

1. day	do	night	say
2. awake	up	play	asleep
3. big	pig	little	boy
4. yes	no	was	girl
5. white	win	frog	black
6. he	the	she	cat
7. sad	happy	mad	and
8. we	see	can	they

Name ___________________________________ skill: categorizing

Draw a line to match each sentence with the correct picture.

I have a cold.

I want something cold.

We saw a tree.

We cut with a saw.

Jim and Bob play.

Kim and Bill are in a play.

Bill is my pet rabbit.

I will pet the rabbit.

I like to paint pictures.

The paint spilled.

Name ______________________ skill: categorizing

Write a sentence for each question using a word from the list that will answer the question logically.

1. What is hot?	ice	chair	sun
The sun is hot.			
2. What can run fast?	turtle	cup	rabbit
3. What can be funny?	clown	tree	dog
4. What is big?	mouse	house	flower
5. What can Father read?	book	ball	apple
6. What will go up?	skate	chair	kite

Name ______________________________ skill: categorizing

Write a sentence for each question using a word from the list that will answer the question logically.

1. What can we do?	run	book	cup
We can run.			
2. What can we eat?	bat	cake	boat
______________________________			
3. What is round like a ball?	sun	window	box
______________________________			
4. What can you play with?	when	truck	grass
______________________________			
5. What can you sit on?	pen	chair	apple
______________________________			
6. What can you put on?	hat	tree	horse
______________________________			

Name ____________________ skill: categorizing

In each row circle the word that does not belong.

1. red	blue	green	hat
2. dog	see	cat	rabbit
3. Bob	Meg	was	Jim
4. home	black	school	store
5. boat	train	bus	when
6. hat	coat	shoes	mouse
7. cookie	tree	cake	candy
8. moon	sun	mother	star

Name ______________________________ skill: categorizing

In each row read each sentence and decide whether or not it is possible. Circle yes or no.

Yes  No

A box can jump.

Children like to play.	Yes	No
A fish can fly.	Yes	No
A tree can read.	Yes	No
Cake is good to eat.	Yes	No
All cats are black.	Yes	No
Ice cream is hot.	Yes	No
Boys and girls go to school.	Yes	No
A book can see.	Yes	No
A rabbit can hop.	Yes	No
Fish can laugh.	Yes	No
Houses can run.	Yes	No
You can ride on a bus.	Yes	No

Name ______________________________ skill: categorizing

What am I?

I am tall. I am green. I have a trunk. What am I? duck house tree man	I am small. I have words. You can read me. What am I? bike book bag cat
I am round. I can roll. Children play with me. What am I? doll book hat ball	I am yellow. I am hot I am in the sky. What am I? sun rain feet snow
I am round. I am silver. I can buy things. What am I? tree ball coin candy	I can hop. I have long ears. I am soft. What am I? cat cow cake rabbit

Name ________________________________ skill: categorizing

In each row circle the words that rhyme with the first word.

1. stop	go	hop	mop	ship	shop
2. play	way	run	may	day	ask
3. see	three	one	tree	not	me
4. make	cake	bake	some	have	lake
5. so	fish	no	party	go	ball
6. then	pen	saw	they	hen	men
7. look	like	took	book	hook	moon
8. sat	mat	on	fat	sit	cat

Name ____________________ skill: categorizing

In each row circle the words that rhyme with the first word.

1. all	fall	fill	ball	tall	am
2. pat	mat	sat	can	bat	pull
3. will	want	Bill	hill	hall	fill
4. car	bar	star	can	far	look
5. man	can	and	fan	now	pan
6. dog	happy	fog	hand	frog	log
7. sad	mad	glad	up	silly	dad
8. fish	wish	fun	dish	stop	me

Name ______________________________ skill: context

In each row circle the word that is almost the same as the underlined word.

1. Bill is a <u>bunny</u>.	bear	rabbit	funny
2. <u>Father</u> is a man.	Mother	Aunt	Dad
3. I live on this <u>road</u>.	street	run	car
4. I was <u>mad</u> when I was lost.	girl	angry	sad
5. The elephant is <u>big</u>.	large	pig	tree
6. The mouse is <u>small</u>.	shoe	sky	tiny
7. I have a pet <u>dog</u>.	cat	puppy	log
8. I live in this <u>house</u>.	home	mouse	key

Name ____________________ skill: context

In each row circle the word that is almost the same as the underlined word.

1. Please have a seat.	chair	sand	hat
2. I can run fast.	slow	fan	quick
3. My mother loves me.	father	mom	pet
4. My hat is on my head.	hot	cap	shoe
5. The water is cool!	cold	pool	can
6. A clown is happy.	old	silly	glad
7. Turn on the lamp.	light	bed	sun
8. We will leave now.	see	go	like

Name ______________________________ skill: context

In each row fill in the blank with the correct word to complete the sentence.

1. Meg________a party.	had	have
2. It________a good party.	was	were
3. Bob and Jim ________.	come	came
4. Peg was________ , too.	there	then
5. They________many games.	play	played
6. Peg said, "________is a good party".	the	this
7. Meg will________the cake.	get	got
8. She________everyone a piece.	give	gives
9. The cake________good.	is	am
10. We all________a good time.	has	had

Name ______________________________ skill: context

In each row fill in the blank with the correct word to complete the sentence.

1. Meg and Peg ________ playing.	are	was
2. They ________ a ball and a rope.	have	has
3. Bob and Jim ________ to play, too.	want	when
4. They want to ________ games.	play	played
5. They can play a fun ________.	game	games
6. They will all ________ fast.	run	ran
7. Bob can run ________ than Jim.	fast	faster
8. He may ________ the race.	win	wins
9. Bob ________ running too soon.	stop	stops
10. Jim ________ the winner.	is	are

Name ______________________________ skill: context

Read the story and answer the questions.

Toad

Bob found an animal. He thought it was a frog. He knew that a frog is green. This animal was brown. A frog is smooth. This animal was bumpy. Bob's animal was really a toad!

1. What did Bob think he found?

____

2. What color was the animal?

____

3. Is a frog brown?

____

4. Was the animal bumpy or smooth?

____

5. Is a frog bumpy or smooth?

____

6. What was Bob's animal?

____

Name ______________________________ skill: context

Read the story and answer the questions.

The Rainbow

It was raining. It had rained all day. Meg wanted to take a walk. She put on her yellow raincoat. She put on her yellow boots. She opened the door and went outside. The rain had stopped and the sun was out. There was a rainbow in the sky.

1. How long had it been raining?

____

2. What did Meg want to do?

____

3. What two things did Meg put on?

____

4. Why did Meg wear boots?

____

5. What happened when Meg went outside?

____

6. Where was the rainbow?

____

Name ____________________ skill: context

Read the story and answer the questions.

The Library

Bob and Meg like to go to the library. There are many books at the library. Bob looks at books about stars and planets. Meg looks at a book about pets. They each pick two books to borrow. They can take the books home for two weeks. Then they must bring the books back.

1. Where did Meg and Bob go?

____

2. What kind of books did Bob look at?

____

3. Meg looked at a book. What was it about?

____

4. What is a library?

____

5. How many books did they each pick?

____

6. Can Meg and Bob keep the books?

7. Name something you can borrow.

____

Name ______________________ skill: context

Read the story and answer the questions.

Camping

Jim and Bob wanted to go camping, but they had no tent. They had an idea. Jim tied a rope between two trees. Bob put an old blanket over the rope. The boys opened the blanket and put heavy rocks on the four corners. They were ready to camp in the backyard.

1. What did the boys want to do?

   ____

2. What did they need?

   ____

3. Where did they make the tent?

   ____

4. Why did they need heavy rocks?

   ____

5. What four things did they use to make the tents?

   ____

6. Why did they need a tent to go camping?

   ____

Answer Key

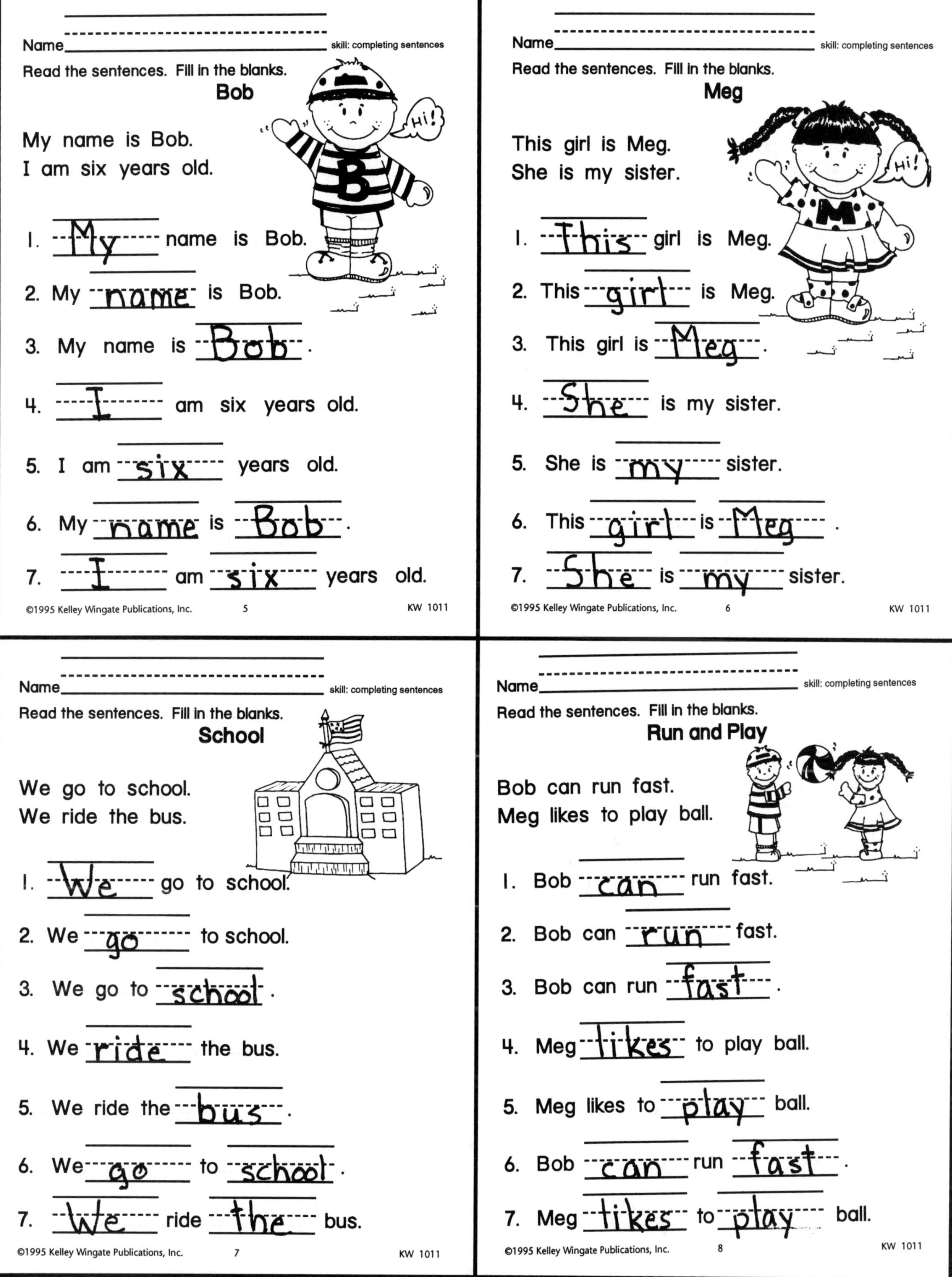

Name ______________________ skill: completing sentences

Read the sentences. Fill in the blanks.

Bob

My name is Bob.
I am six years old.

1. My name is Bob.
2. My name is Bob.
3. My name is Bob.
4. I am six years old.
5. I am six years old.
6. My name is Bob.
7. I am six years old.

 5 KW 1011

Name ______________________ skill: completing sentences

Read the sentences. Fill in the blanks.

Meg

This girl is Meg.
She is my sister.

1. This girl is Meg.
2. This girl is Meg.
3. This girl is Meg.
4. She is my sister.
5. She is my sister.
6. This girl is Meg.
7. She is my sister.

 6 KW 1011

Name ______________________ skill: completing sentences

Read the sentences. Fill in the blanks.

School

We go to school.
We ride the bus.

1. We go to school.
2. We go to school.
3. We go to school.
4. We ride the bus.
5. We ride the bus.
6. We go to school.
7. We ride the bus.

 7 KW 1011

Name ______________________ skill: completing sentences

Read the sentences. Fill in the blanks.

Run and Play

Bob can run fast.
Meg likes to play ball.

1. Bob can run fast.
2. Bob can run fast.
3. Bob can run fast.
4. Meg likes to play ball.
5. Meg likes to play ball.
6. Bob can run fast.
7. Meg likes to play ball.

 8 KW 1011

Answer Key

Name ______________________ skill: completing sentences

Read the sentences. Fill in the blanks.

Miss Snow

Miss Snow works at school.
She helps Meg and Bob read.

1. Miss Snow works at school.
2. Miss Snow works at school.
3. Miss Snow works at school.
4. She helps Meg and Bob read.
5. She helps Meg and Bob read.
6. Miss Snow works at school.
7. She helps Meg and Bob read.

Name ______________________ skill: completing sentences

Read the sentences. Fill in the blanks.

Bill

Our class has a pet.
His name is Bill.

1. Our class has a pet.
2. Our class has a pet.
3. Our class has a pet.
4. His name is Bill.
5. His name is Bill.
6. Our class has a pet.
7. His name is Bill.

Name ______________________ skill: completing sentences

Read the sentences. Fill in the blanks.

A Fish

This fish is funny.
It is blue and yellow.

1. This fish is funny.
2. This fish is funny.
3. It is blue and yellow.
4. It is blue and yellow.
5. It is blue and yellow.
6. This fish is funny.
7. It is blue and yellow.

Name ______________________ skill: completing sentences

Read the sentences. Fill in the blanks.

Ready To Go

We will go home soon.
Get ready to go!

1. We will go home soon.
2. We will go home soon.
3. We will go home soon.
4. We will go home soon.
5. Get ready to go!
6. Get ready to go!
7. Get ready to go!

Answer Key

Name ______________________ skill: completing sentences

Read the sentences. Fill in the blanks.

Mother

Mother is at the bus stop.
She walks us home.

1. Mother is at the bus stop.
2. Mother is at the bus stop.
3. Mother is at the bus stop.
4. She walks us home.
5. She walks us home.
6. She walks us home.
7. She walks us home.

 13 KW 1011

Name ______________________ skill: completing sentences

Read the sentences. Fill in the blanks.

Good Cookies

We will eat something now.
Cookies and milk are good!

1. We will eat something now.
2. We will eat something now.
3. Cookies and milk are good!
4. Cookies and milk are good!
5. Cookies and milk are good!
6. We will eat something now.
7. Cookies and milk are good!

 14 KW 1011

Name ______________________ skill: answering questions

Read the story and answer the questions.

Jim

Jim is Bob's friend.
They play with trains and trucks.
They make up games with these toys.

1. Who is Jim?
   Bob's friend
2. Who is Bob's friend?
   Jim
3. Who plays with trains and trucks?
   Jim and Bob
4. What toys do Jim and Bob play with?
   trains and trucks
5. Are apples and cookies toys?
   no

 15 KW 1011

Name ______________________ skill: answering questions

Read the story and answer the questions.

Peg

Peg comes to play with Meg.
She has a big blue bike.
Meg has some green skates and a doll.

1. Who comes to play with Meg?
   Peg
2. What does Peg's bike look like?
   It is big and blue.
3. What color are the skates?
   green
4. Who has the doll?
   Meg
5. What two toys does Meg have?
   skates and a doll

 16 KW 1011

Answer Key

Name________________ skill: answering questions

Read the story and answer the questions.

The Race

Peg had a race with Jim.
They ran from the tree to the sidewalk.
Peg fell down and Jim won the race.

1. Who had a race?
   Peg and Jim
2. Where did they run?
   from the tree to the sidewalk
3. Who fell down?
   Peg
4. Who won the race?
   Jim
5. Why did Peg lose the race?
   because she fell down

Name________________ skill: beginning reading-answering questions

Read the story and answer the questions.

A Party

The children had a party.
The boys blew up balloons.
The girls gave cake to everyone.
They laughed and had fun.

1. What did the children have?
   a party
2. Who had the party?
   the children
3. Who blew up the balloons?
   the boys
4. What did the girls do?
   gave cake to everyone
5. What did they do at the party?
   they laughed and had fun

Name________________ skill: answering questions

Read the story and answer the questions.

The Surprise

Meg and Peg hid behind the tree.
Bob and Jim were walking across the yard
The girls jumped out from behind the tree.
The boys were very surprised!

1. Where did the girls hide?
   behind the tree
2. Who was walking across the yard?
   Bob and Jim
3. What did the girls do first?
   hid behind the tree
4. Who was surprised?
   the boys
5. How did the girls surprise the boys?
   jumped out from behind the tree

Name________________ skill: answering questions

Read the story and answer the questions.

Train

Bob was playing with his train.
The train fell off the table.
A wheel was broken.
Father helped Bob fix train.

1. What was Bob playing with?
   his train
2. Whose train was it?
   Bob's train
3. What happened to the train?
   it fell off the table
4. What was broken?
   a wheel
5. Who helped Bob?
   Father

Answer Key

Name
skill: beginning reading-answering questions

Read the story and answer the questions.

The Book

Meg was reading a big brown book.
The book was about a little girl and her cat.
The girl was named Evie.
The cat was named Socks because he had black feet.
Meg liked the story very much.

1. What color was the book?
   brown
2. What was the story about?
   a little girl and her cat
3. Who was Evie?
   the girl in the book
4. Why was the cat named Socks?
   he had black feet
5. Was Socks a boy or a girl?
   a boy
6. Did Meg like the book?
   yes

 21 CD-3708

Name
skill: beginning reading-answering questions

Read the story and answer the questions.

School Play

One day there was a funny play at school.
Bob and Jim were clowns.
Peg and Meg were lions.
All the mothers and fathers came to see it.
They laughed and clapped when it was over.

1. What did the mothers and fathers come to see?
   a play
2. Who were clowns?
   Bob and Jim
3. What were Peg and Meg?
   lions
4. Where was the play?
   at school
5. Did the mothers and fathers like the play?
   yes
6. What did they do when it was over?
   laughed and clapped

 22 CD-3708

Name
skill: answering questions

Read the story and answer the questions.

On the Farm

Mother and Father took Meg and Bob to a farm.
There were many baby animals to pet.
Meg fed a little white goat.
Bob rode a tall brown horse.
The wagon ride was the most fun of all.

1. Where did Meg and Bob go?
   to a farm
2. What did they pet?
   baby animals
3. Who fed the goat?
   Meg
4. What was the most fun of all?
   the wagon ride
5. What did the goat look like?
   it was little and white
6. What did Bob ride on?
   a tall brown horse

 23 KW 1011

Name
skill: answering questions

Read the story and answer the questions.

Fishing

It was a warm and sunny day.
Bob and Jim went fishing at the pond.
Jim caught a green fish and a yellow fish.
Bob caught a large black fish.
The boys let their fish go.
They wanted to catch the fish again some other day.

1. Where did Bob and Jim go?
   fishing at the pond
2. Who caught the large black fish?
   Bob
3. What did the boys do with their fish?
   they let them go
4. What did Jim catch?
   a green fish and a yellowfish
5. What kind of day was it?
   warm and sunny
6. Why did they let the fish go?
   to catch them again anotherday
7. Who caught the most fish?
   Jim

 24 KW 1011

Answer Key

Name____________________ skill: beginning reading-answering questions

Read the story and answer the questions.

Matt the Bat

Matt is a bat. He has many pals to play with. They all go to school. It is a bat school. He learns to fly. He likes to read books, too!

1. What is Matt?
   a bat
2. What does Matt do with his pals?
   he plays with his pals
3. Where do they go?
   to school
4. What school do they go to?
   a bat school
5. What does Matt do at school?
   learns to fly
6. What does Matt like to do?
   read books
7. Is this story real or make-believe?
   make-believe

 25 CD-3708

Name____________________ skill: answering questions

Read the story and answer the questions.

The Little Egg

Mother Hen had one little egg. She sat on it for many days. The other hens said her egg was too little. It was not a good egg. Mother Hen did not listen. One day the little egg opened. Out came the biggest chick of all!

1. What did Mother Hen have?
   a little egg
2. How long did she sit on it?
   for many days
3. What did the other hens say?
   it was too little
4. Was the egg good?
   yes
5. Did Mother Hen listen to the others?
   no
6. What came out of the little egg?
   a big chick
7. Can hens talk?
   no

 26 KW 1011

Name____________________ skill: answering questions

Read the story and answer the questions.

Ben

Ben the puppy wanted to play. No one was home. Jim was at school. Ben looked in his box. There was a ball. There was a sock. But there was no one to play with. Ben was sad. The door opened. Jim was home!

1. Who was Ben?
   a puppy
2. What did he want to do?
   to play
3. Who was home?
   no one
4. Where was Jim?
   at school
5. What was in Ben's box?
   a ball, a sock
6. How did Ben feel?
   sad
7. How did Ben feel when Jim came home?
   happy

 27 KW 1011

Name____________________ skill: answering questions

Read the story and answer the questions.

Sue

Sue is a skunk. She likes children. She wants to play with them. Children run away from her. They are afraid. This makes Sue very sad, but she has a plan. Today Sue will go to the zoo. She will ask if she can stay there. Do you think Sue can stay?

1. Who is Sue?
   a skunk
2. What does Sue like to do?
   play with children
3. What do children do when they see Sue?
   run away
4. Why do they run away?
   they are afraid
5. Where will Sue go?
   to the zoo
6. What will Sue ask at the zoo?
   if she can stay
7. Is this story real or make-believe?
   make-believe

 28 KW 1011

Answer Key

Name ____________________ skill: answering questions
Read the story and answer the questions.

Lenny

Lenny was a big cat. One day a man took him away. He put Lenny in the circus. Why put a cat in the circus? Lenny did not know. Each day Lenny grew bigger. He learned new tricks. One day Lenny tried to meow. Out came a big roar. "What a good joke," said Lenny. "I am really a lion!"

1. What did Lenny think he was?
   a cat
2. Where did the man take Lenny?
   to the circus
3. What did Lenny do each day?
   he grew bigger
4. What did Lenny learn?
   new tricks
5. What happened when he tried to meow?
   he roared
6. What was Lenny really?
   a lion
7. Is this story real or make-believe?
   make-believe

 29 KW 1011

Name ____________________ skill: answering questions

Finding Food

Boo was a bear cub. Every morning he went with his mother to find food. He was not much help to Mother. He liked to play with the flowers and other baby animals. One day Boo saw a hole in a tree. He stuck in his paw. It was very sticky. Boo had found a honey hive!

1. What is the little bear's name?
   Boo
2. What does he do every morning?
   go with his Mother
3. Why isn't Boo much help?
   he likes to play
4. What did he see one day?
   a hole in a tree
5. What did he do?
   stuck in his paw
6. What had Boo found?
   a honey hive

 30 KW 1011

Name ____________________ skill: answering questions
Read the story and answer the questions.

Going to the Moon

We like to go to the moon. We go there every Saturday. The moon has lots of dust and rocks. I like to jump because I can go so high. My sister picks up rocks to bring home. We get back just in time for lunch.

1. Where do we like to go?
   to the Moon
2. What day do we go there?
   Saturday
3. What is on the moon?
   dust and rocks.
4. Who picks up rocks?
   my sister
5. What do I like to do?
   jump
6. When do we get back?
   in time for lunch
7. Is this story real or make-believe?
   make-believe

 31 KW 1011

Name ____________________ skill: answering questions
Read the story and answer the questions.

Randy

Randy was a red race car. He did not care about driving fast. He did not care about winning the race. He liked to go slow. He wanted to look at everything as he went. Randy never won a race, but he had a lot of fun.

1. What is the name of the race car?
   Randy
2. What color is he?
   red
3. How does he like to drive?
   slow
4. Did he care when he lost?
   no
5. What does Randy like to do when he drives?
   look at everything
6. How many races has Randy won?
   none
7. Is this story real or make-believe?
   make-believe

 32 KW 1011

Answer Key

Name ____________ skill: answering questions
Read the story and answer the questions.

Under the Sea

If I could live anywhere it would be under the sea. I would live in a glass house so I could watch the fish. I would grow seaweed to eat. I would ride seahorses to school. The fish would be my best friends. You could come to see me. You would get wet!

1. Where would I like to live?
   under the sea
2. What would my house be made of?
   glass
3. What food would I eat?
   seaweed
4. How would I get to school?
   seahorses
5. Who would be my friends?
   the fish
6. Is this story real or make-believe?
   make-believe

Name ____________ skill: answering questions
Read the story and answer the questions.

Jill the Giant

Jill was a giant. She was the only giant in Little Town. Poor Jill. The children were afraid of her. She was too big. One day she saw a boy named John in a tree. He could not get down. Jill helped John. She took him from the tree and put him on the ground. Then the children liked her.

1. What was Jill?
   a giant
2. Why were the children afraid of her?
   she was big
3. Who was in the tree?
   John
4. What was wrong with John?
   he could not get down.
5. What did Jill do?
   She helped him
6. How did the children feel after that?
   they liked her
7. Is this story real or make-believe?
   make believe

Name ____________ skill: answering questions
Read the story and answer the questions.

Bats

There is a bat in this cave. He is sleeping. He holds on with his feet. Bats sleep all day. They fly out of the cave at night. They eat bugs that fly.

1. What is in the cave?
   a bat
2. What is the bat doing?
   sleeping
3. How does he hold on?
   with his feet
4. When do bats go out of the cave?
   at night
5. What do bats eat?
   bugs
6. Name another animal that sleeps all day.
   ____

Name ____________ skill: answering questions
Read the story and answer the questions.

Chicken Eggs

Chickens are birds. The hens lay eggs. They sit on the eggs to warm them. The baby chicks grow inside the eggs. When the chick is ready it pecks at the shell. Out pops a new chick!

1. What are chickens?
   birds
2. Who lays the eggs?
   hens
3. How do they keep the eggs warm?
   they sit on them
4. What grows inside the egg?
   baby chicks
5. When does the chick come out?
   when it is ready
6. Name another animal that lays eggs.
   ____

Answer Key

Name ______________________ skill: answering questions
Read the story and answer the questions.

The Zoo

Many wild animals live at the zoo. Brown bears eat fish. Lions sleep in the sun. Seals splash playfully in the water. Most children like the monkeys best. The zoo is fun!

1. Where do many wild animals live?
   at the zoo
2. What does the bear eat?
   fish
3. Which animals do most children like best?
   monkeys
4. What do the seals like to do?
   splash in the water
5. Who sleeps in the sun?
   lions
6. Name another animal you can see at the zoo.
   ____

Name ______________________ skill: answering questions
Read the story and answer the questions.

The Circus

The circus is not like a zoo. Circus animals can do tricks. Bears dance and ride bikes. Tigers jump through hoops. People also do tricks. Some swing high in the air. The clowns make everyone laugh. It is a good show!

1. What is this story about?
   the circus
2. What animal rides a bike?
   bears
3. Where do tigers jump?
   through the hoops
4. What do the bears do?
   dance, ride bikes
5. What tricks can people do?
   swing in the air
6. Draw a picture of the third sentence.

Name ______________________ skill: answering questions
Read the story and answer the questions.

A Good Star

The sun is a star. It is far from where we live. The sun looks like a big ball. It is very hot. We need the sun's light. It keeps us warm. It helps plants grow. The sun is a good star for us.

1. What is this story about?
   the sun
2. What is the sun?
   a star
3. What does the sun look like?
   a big ball
4. What does the sun feel like?
   it is very hot
5. How does the sun help us?
   it keeps us warm
6. How does the sun help plants?
   it helps them grow

Name ______________________ skill: answering questions
Read the story and answer the questions.

Trees

Trees are the biggest plant of all. They have roots in the dirt. The roots take in water. Trees have leaves. The leaves use sunlight to make food. We sit in the shade under trees. We use the wood to make many things.

1. What are the biggest plants?
   trees
2. Where are the roots?
   in the dirt
3. How does a tree get water?
   from the roots
4. Why do the leaves need sunlight?
   to make food
5. What do we use the wood for?
   to make many things

Answer Key

Name ____________________ skill: answering questions

Read the story and answer the questions.

Ways to Go

We have lots of ways to go places. We ride on bikes on sidewalks. Cars and buses drive on roads. Boats and ships sail on water. Airplanes and rockets fly in the air. Each trip can take us somewhere new.

1. What do we ride on sidewalks?
   bikes
2. Where do boats and ships sail?
   on water
3. What do cars and buses do?
   drive on roads
4. What can fly in the air?
   Airplanes and rockets
5. What is this story about?
   transportation
6. How did you get to school this morning?
   ____

Name ____________________ skill: answering questions

Read the story and answer the questions.

Beavers

Beavers live in ponds. They have sharp teeth. They can cut down small trees. These trees are put into the pond to make a home. Beavers live with their families. Their flat tail helps them swim.

1. What is this story about?
   beavers
2. Where do beavers live?
   in ponds
3. What do beavers make out of trees?
   a home
4. How do they cut the trees?
   with their teeth
5. Who do beavers live with?
   their families
6. Why do beavers have flat tails?
   it helps them swim

Name ____________________ skill: answering questions

Read the story and answer the questions.

Bears

Bears are big animals. They have fur to keep them warm. They have short tails. Bears can stand on their back feet. Then they are very tall! Most bears eat plants and bugs. In the fall they eat a lot. Then bears can sleep all winter.

1. What is this story about?
   bears
2. When are bears very tall?
   when they stand up
3. Do bears have a long tail?
   no
4. What do bears eat?
   plants and bugs
5. Why do bears eat a lot in the fall?
   because they sleep all winter
6. What keeps bears warm?
   their fur

Name ____________________ skill: following directions

Read then do.

Here is a barn.
Color the barn red.
Draw three eggs near it.

(red)

Here is a book.
Write the word "read" on it.
Color the book blue.

(blue) read MUSIC

Here is a cat.
Color the cat orange.
Draw a ball near the cat.

(orange)

Here is a big truck.
Color the truck red.
Draw a blue ball on the truck.

(red)

Answer Key

Name ____________ skill: following directions
Read then do.

Here is a hen.
Color the hen brown.
Draw three eggs near it.

Here is a sock.
Color it black.
Draw another sock near it.

(black)

Here is a box.
Draw a green ball in it.
Color the box orange.

(orange)

Here is a fish.
Color it yellow.
Draw three little fish near it.

(yellow)

 45 KW 1011

Name ____________ skill: following directions
Read then do.

Here are three books.
They are on the table.
Color two books green.
Put an X on one book.

Bill is here.
His dog is here, too.
Color the dog brown.
Draw a line under Bill.

(brown)

Here is the school bus.
Two girls are on the bus.
Put an X on the bus.
Circle one of the girls.

Here is a barn.
A cow is near the barn.
Put an X on the cow.
Draw a line under the barn.

 46 KW 1011

Name ____________ skill: following directions
Read then do.

Here is a glass of milk.
It is on the table.
Draw a cookie near the glass.
Circle the glass of milk.

Here is a bed.
A cat is on the bed.
Put an X on the cat.
Circle the cat.

Here are three balls.
Color the biggest one green.
Put a line under the smallest one.
Put an X on the one with a star.

(green)

Here are three boxes.
Color the last one green.
Put an X on the first one.
Put a line under the biggest one.

(green)

 47 KW 1011

Name ____________ skill: following directions
Read then draw a zoo.

Draw a big pool.
Draw a seal near the pool.
Color the seal black or brown.
Draw a tree near the pool.
Draw a monkey near the tree.
Draw something for the monkey to eat.
Draw one more animal near the pool.

 48 KW 1011

Answer Key

Name____________________ skill: following directions

Read then draw a farm.

Draw a big barn.
Color the barn red.
Draw two ducks near the barn.
Color the ducks white or yellow.
Draw a cow in the barn.
Draw a white and brown horse near the barn.
Draw a girl on the horse.

 49 KW 1011

Name____________________ skill: sequencing

1. Read the story.

Baking a Cake

Meg is making a cake. She puts everything she needs into the bowl. Then she mixes the batter. The batter goes into the oven to bake. Soon it smells good.

2. Read the sentences below. Rewrite them in the correct order on the lines below.

Mix the batter.
The cake is baked.
Put everything in the bowl.
Put the batter in the oven.

1. Put everything in the bowl.
2. Mix the batter.
3. Put the batter in the oven.
4. The cake is baked.

 50 KW 1011

Name____________________ skill: sequencing

1. Read the story.

Pet Fish

I have three pet fish. When I tap on the glass they swim to the top. I give them their food. I feed them until they are full. They wave their tails as they swim away.

2. Read the sentences below. Rewrite them in the correct order on the lines below.

They eat until they are full.
I tap on the glass.
I drop their food into the bowl.
They wave their tails.

1. I tap on the glass.
2. I drop their food into the bou
3. They eat until they are full.
4. They wave their tails.

 51 KW 1011

Name____________________ skill: sequencing

1. Read the story.

Ready for School

It is time for school. I ate my eggs and toast. I drank my juice. I washed my face then brushed my teeth. I got dressed before the bus came.

2. Read the sentences below. Rewrite them in the correct order on the lines below.

Get dressed.
Eat breakfast.
Brush your teeth.
Wash your face.

1. Eat breakfast.
2. Wash your face.
3. Brush your teeth.
4. Get dressed.

 52 KW 1011

Answer Key

Name ______________________ skill: sequencing

1. Read the story.

Making Lunch

Sue will fix her own lunch. First, she will open the can of soup. Then she heats the soup on the stove. It tastes good. Last, Sue cleans the dishes.

2. Read the sentences below. Rewrite them in the correct order on the lines below.

Open up the soup.
Clean up the dishes.
Eat the soup.
Heat up the soup.

1. Open up the soup.
2. Heat up the soup.
3. Eat the soup.
4. Clean up the dishes.

Name ______________________ skill: sequencing

1. Read the story.

Plant a Seed

We planted some apple seeds. We watered them every day. They grew into small plants. Now they are small trees. Someday we will eat the apples that grow on them.

2. Read the sentences below. Rewrite them in the correct order on the lines below.

We watered the seeds.
We have small apple trees.
We planted some apple seeds.
Small plants grew from the seeds.

1. We planted some apple seeds.
2. We watered the seeds.
3. Small plants grew from the seeds.
4. We have small apple trees.

Name ______________________ skill: sequencing

1. Read the story.

New Clothes

Ted needed some new clothes. He needed socks, shoes, and shirts. He made a list of what he needed to buy. Mother drove him to the store. They found all the things on his list then paid for them.

2. Read the sentences below. Rewrite them in the correct order on the lines below.

Ted made a list of what he needed.
Mother took him to the store.
Ted paid for the new clothes.
They found everything on the list.

1. Ted made a list of what he needed.
2. Mother took him to the store.
3. They found everything on the list.
4. Ted paid for the new clothes.

Name ______________________ skill: sequencing

1. Read the story.

Soccer

Today was my first soccer lesson. The teacher said, "My name is Beth. I will be your teacher. Please sit down on the grass." We learned how to kick the ball. It was fun.

2. Read the sentences below. Rewrite them in the correct order on the lines below.

"My name is Beth"
I learned to kick the ball.
"Please sit down."
Today I had a soccer lesson.

1. Today I had a soccer lesson.
2. "My name is Beth"
3. "Please sit down."
4. I learned to kick the ball.

Answer Key

Name ______________________ skill: sequencing

1. Read the story.

The Letter

Ann got a new bike for her birthday. Grandpa gave it to her. Ann wrote a thank-you letter. She mailed the letter. After he opened the letter, Grandpa read it. He was very happy.

2. Read the sentences below. Rewrite them in the correct order on the lines below.

Ann wrote a letter.
Grandpa opened the letter.
Ann got a new bike.
Ann mailed the letter.
Grandpa was happy.

1. Ann got a new bike.
2. Ann wrote a letter.
3. Ann mailed the letter.
4. Grandpa opened the letter.
5. Grandpa was happy.

 57 KW 1011

Name ______________________ skill: sequencing

1. Read the story.

Swimming

I have on my swimsuit. Let's go to your house to play. We can run in the sprinkler. Then we can swim in the pool. We will dry off on the big brown towels and then have lunch.

2. Read the sentences below. Rewrite them in the correct order on the lines below.

We can have lunch.
We can get wet in the sprinkler.
We will use towels to dry off.
We will go to your house.
We will go in the pool.

1. We will go to your house.
2. We can get wet in the sprinkl
3. We will go in the pool.
4. We will use towels to dry off
5. We can have lunch.

 58 KW 1011

Name ______________________ skill: sequencing

1. Read the story.

Make a Kite

Today we made a kite. Susan had the sticks. Peter cut the paper to fit. Jack pasted it together. I put on the string then the tail. Let's go fly a kite.

2. Read the sentences below. Rewrite them in the correct order on the lines below.

Fly the kite.
Lay the paper on the sticks.
Put on string and a tail.
We want to make a kite.
Paste the paper on the sticks.

1. We want to make a kite.
2. Lay the paper on the sticks
3. Paste the paper on the sticks.
4. Put on string and a tail.
5. Fly the kite.

 59 KW 1011

Name ______________________ skill: sequencing

1. Read the story.

Ready to Go

"We must hurry," said Mother. "We are almost late." I put on my socks. Mother tied my shoes. We brushed my hair then put a ribbon in it. Mother started the car. Now we are ready.

2. Read the sentences below. Rewrite them in the correct order on the lines below.

I put my socks and shoes on.
Mother put a ribbon in my hair.
My hair was brushed.
We are ready to go.
Mother started the car.

1. I put my socks and shoes on.
2. My hair was brushed.
3. Mother put a ribbon in my hair.
4. Mother started the car.
5. We are ready to go.

 60 KW 1011

Answer Key

Name ______________________ skill: sequencing

1. Read the story.

Go to Bed

Every night Max gets ready for bed. First he takes a bath in the tub. Next he gets out the toothbrush and paste. He brushes up and down very well. Then Father reads a good-night story to him. Last, Max closes his eyes and goes to sleep.

2. Read the sentences below. Rewrite them in the correct order on the lines below.

Father reads a story.
Max brushes his teeth.
Max closes his eyes.
He gets out the toothbrush.
Max takes a bath.

1. Max takes a bath.
2. He gets out the toothbrush.
3. Max brushes his teeth.
4. Father reads a story.
5. Max closes his eyes.

 61 KW 1011

Name ______________________ skill: sequencing

1. Read the story.

The Snake

There is a little snake in my yard. He lives under the rose bush. He eats flies and other bugs. My mother does not mind having him there. She says he is helpful. I call the snake Stripes. He is kind of like a pet to me.

2. Read the sentences below. Rewrite them in the correct order on the lines below.

He lives under a bush.
Mother says he is helpful.
We have a snake in our yard.
He is like a pet.
The snake eats flies and bugs.

1. We have a snake in our yard.
2. He lives under a bush.
3. The snake eats flies and bugs.
4. Mother says he is helpful.
5. He is like a pet.

 62 CD-3708

Name ______________________ skill: sequencing

1. Read the story.

Pizza

Pizza is my favorite food. Mother calls the store and tells them what we want. Soon someone brings it to our door. It smells so good! Father cuts the pieces and puts them on a plate. I can eat three or four pieces because I really like it.

2. Read the sentences below. Rewrite them in the correct order on the lines below.

Someone brings it to our door.
I eat many pieces.
Father cuts the pizza.
Mother calls to order the pizza.
He puts the pieces on our plates.

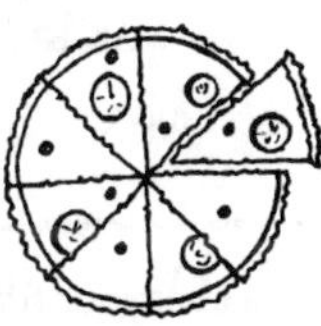

1. Mother calls to order the pizza.
2. Someone brings it to our door.
3. Father cuts the pizza.
4. He puts the pieces on our plate.
5. I eat many pieces.

 63 KW 1011

Name ______________________ skill: "s" endings

In each row choose the correct description for each picture and write it in the blank.

Answer	Choices	Answer
one kitten	one kitten / two kittens / three kittens	two kittens
three balls	one ball / two balls / three balls	two balls
two books	one book / two books / three books	one book
two boys	one boy / two boys / three boys	three boys
one box	one box / two boxes / three boxes	three boxes

 64 KW 1011

Answer Key

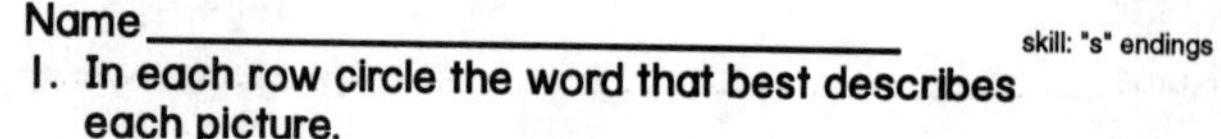

Name______________________ skill: "s" endings

1. In each row circle the word that best describes each picture.

2. Draw a little red house with two green trees near it.

© 1995 Kelley Wingate Publications, Inc. 65 KW 1011

Name______________________ skill: "s" endings

Choose the correct word for each sentence.

1. I can come to the party. Jim comes to my house. come comes	2. Peg wants to be alone. We want a cookie. want wants
3. She will give it to me. He gives me one. give gives	4. Meg can see the play. She sees a dog. see sees
5. Who runs fast? We run fast. run runs	6. I laugh at a joke. She laughs a lot. laugh laughs
7. Bob jumps high. Jim can jump higher. jump jumps	8. I hop on one foot. She hops over a ball. hop hops

© 1995 Kelley Wingate Publications, Inc. 66 KW 1011

Name______________________ skill: "s" endings

Circle the correct word in each box.

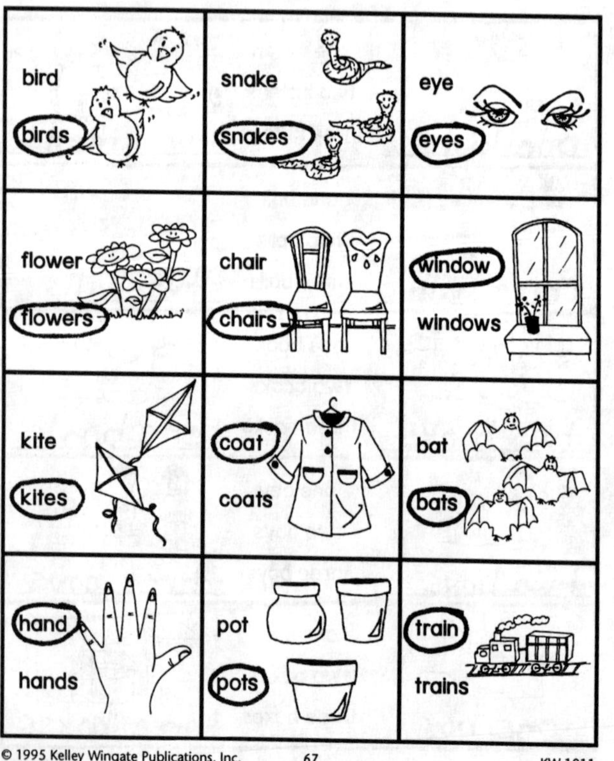

© 1995 Kelley Wingate Publications, Inc. 67 KW 1011

Name______________________ skill: "es" endings

Choose the correct word for each sentence.

1. I have a box. There are two boxes. box boxes	2. The fox is red. Three foxes are red. fox foxes
3. I made two wishes today. I made a wish on a star. wish wishes	4. Lunches are fun to make! What is for lunch? lunch Lunches
5. Wash your hands. Beth washes the dishes. Wash washes	6. That mixes me up! Please mix the cards. mix mixes
7. Father fixes the tire. I can help fix it. fix fixes	8. Will you watch the play? Bob watches with us. watch watches

© 1995 Kelley Wingate Publications, Inc. 68 KW 1011

Answer Key

Name ______________________ skill: "er" endings

Fill in the blank with the correct word.

1. The dog is bigger than the cat.	big	bigger
2. The bird is higher than the house.	high	higher
3. It is a hot day.	hot	hotter
4. The bear is very fat.	fat	fatter
5. I have a small puppy.	small	smaller
6. He is a tall boy.	tall	taller
7. Her dress is longer than yours.	long	longer
8. I am a fast runner.	fast	faster
9. The turtle is slower than the rabbit.	slow	slower
10. That was a short story.	short	shorter

© 1995 Kelley Wingate Publications, Inc. 69 KW 1011

Name ______________________ skill: "ed" endings

Fill in the blank with the correct word.

1. Jim looked for the ball.	look	looked
2. Meg can jump high.	jump	jumped
3. Bob helped his father.	help	helped
4. We want to go now.	want	wanted
5. Peg likes to work at school.	work	worked
6. I will play tonight.	play	played
7. Mother liked my picture.	like	liked
8. The funny play made us laugh.	laugh	laughed
9. Mother washed the dish.	wash	washed
10. Peg will walk to the store.	walk	walked

© 1995 Kelley Wingate Publications, Inc. 70 KW 1011

Name ______________________ skill: "er" or "ed"

Fill in the blank with the correct word.

1. Meg smiled at Peg and Jim.	smile	smiled
2. They were near home.	near	neared
3. It was darker than before.	dark	darker
4. They saw a brown bat!	brown	browner
5. Meg handed the light to Jim.	hand	handed
6. Bill hopped across the grass.	hop	hopped
7. He loved to eat grass.	love	loved
8. Peg will take care of Bill.	care	cared
9. Meg will show Peg how.	show	showed
10. They had a great time!	great	greater

© 1995 Kelley Wingate Publications, Inc. 71 KW 1011

Name ______________________ skill: "ed" endings

Fill in the blank with the correct word.

1. The cake is baked.	bake	baked
2. The children will start now.	start	started
3. We have moved to a new house.	move	moved
4. His name is Bill.	name	named
5. I will take a trip soon.	trip	tripped
6. Peg is a good dancer.	dance	dancer
7. Jim can trick the others.	trick	tricked
8. Meg is a talker in class!	talk	talker
9. Mr. Brown can bake cakes.	bake	baker
10. Bob is faster than Jim.	fast	faster

© 1995 Kelley Wingate Publications, Inc. 72 KW 1011

Answer Key

Name______________________________ skill: recognizing beginning consonants

In each box draw a line to match the letter to the picture that begins with that letter.

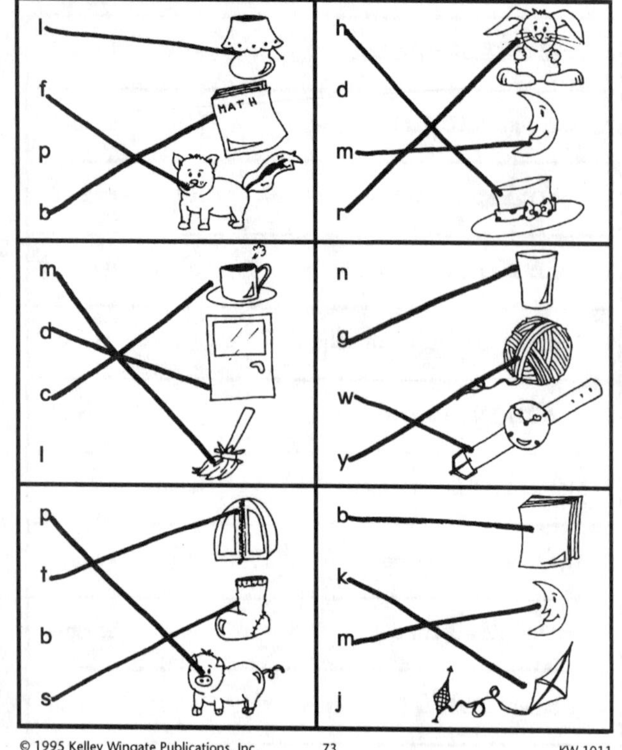

 73 KW 1011

Name______________________________ skill: recognizing beginning consonants

In each box draw a line to match the letter to the picture that begins with that letter.

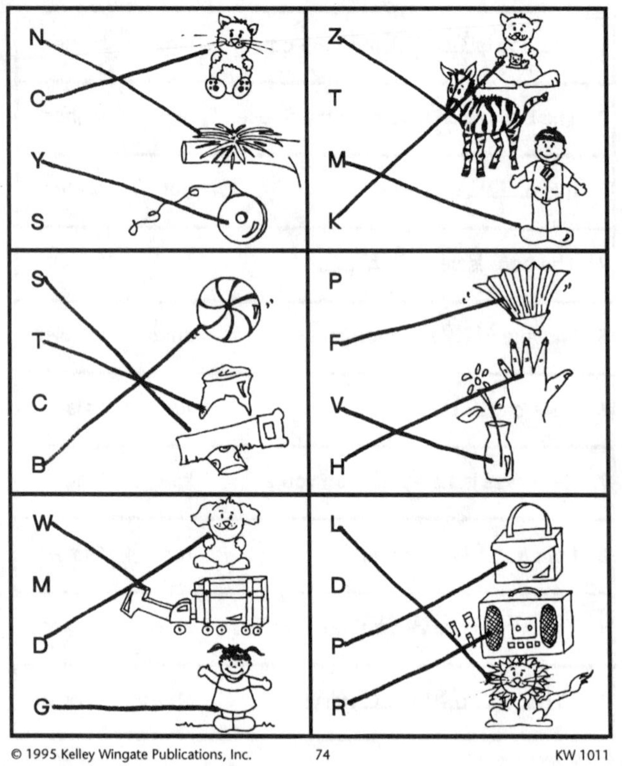

 74 KW 1011

Name______________________________ skill: recognizing beginning consonants

In each box circle the picture that begins with the same letter as the letter at the top of the box.

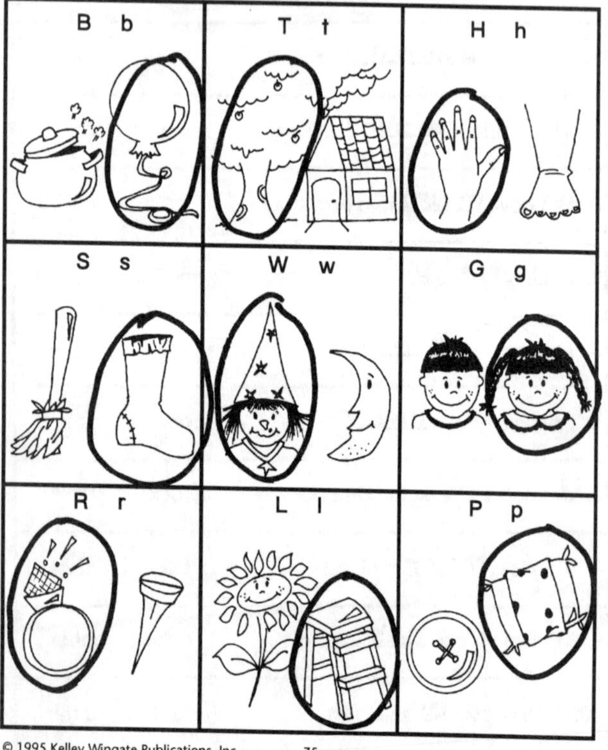

 75 KW 1011

Name______________________________ skill: recognizing beginning consonants

In each box circle the letter that the picture begins with.

 76 KW 1011

Answer Key

Name__________________________________ skill: recognizing ending consonants

In each box draw a line to match the letter to the picture that ends with the same letter.

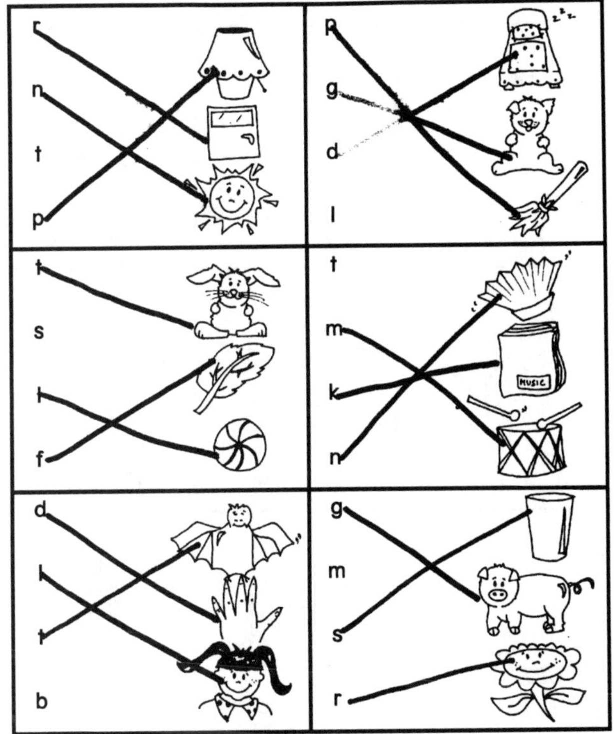

 77 KW 1011

Name__________________________________ skill: recognizing ending consonants

In each box draw a line to match the letter to the picture that ends with the same letter.

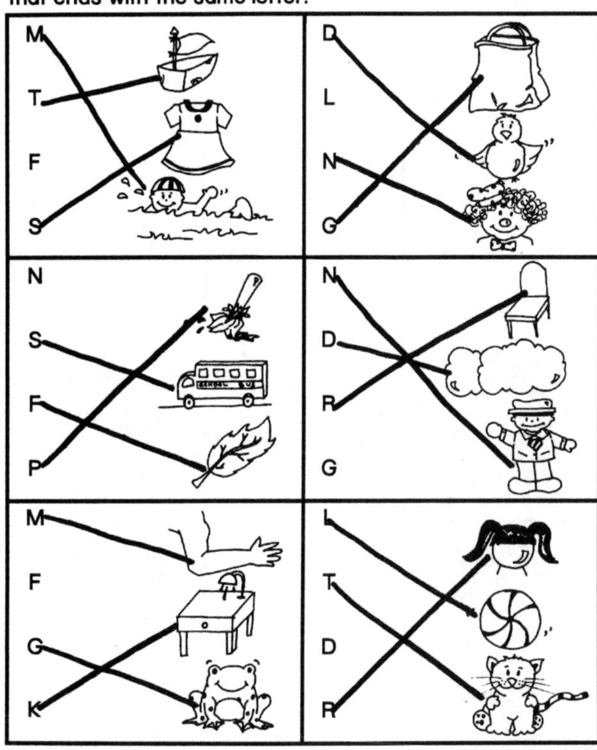

 78 KW 1011

Name__________________________________ skill: recognizing ending consonants

In each box draw a line to match the letter to the picture that ends with the same letter.

 79 KW 1011

Name__________________________________ skill: recognizing ending consonants

In each box draw a line to match the letter to the picture that ends with the same letter.

 80 KW 1011

Answer Key

Name ______________________ skill: recognizing beginning and ending consonants

In each box fill in the blanks to complete the word.

BALL	STAR	DUCK
MAN	DOG	BUS
COAT	PAIL	BOAT

 81 KW 1011

Name ______________________ skill: recognizing beginning and ending consonants

In each box fill in the blanks to complete the word.

BOOK	BIRD	WINDOW
FLOWER	SUN	FISH
TRAIN	CAKE	WIND

 82 KW 1011

Name ______________________ skill: categorizing

In each row circle the word that is the opposite of the first word.

1. boy	boat	go	(girl)
2. hot	(cold)	see	hat
3. up	barn	(down)	on
4. sun	now	was	(moon)
5. on	ball	top	(off)
6. stop	hop	(go)	dog
7. went	(came)	her	sent
8. hello	yellow	sun	(good-by)

 83 KW 1011

Name ______________________ skill: categorizing

In each row circle the word that is the opposite of the first word.

1. day	do	(night)	say
2. awake	up	play	(asleep)
3. big	pig	(little)	boy
4. yes	(no)	was	girl
5. white	win	frog	(black)
6. he	the	(she)	cat
7. sad	(happy)	mad	and
8. we	see	can	(they)

 84 KW 1011

Answer Key

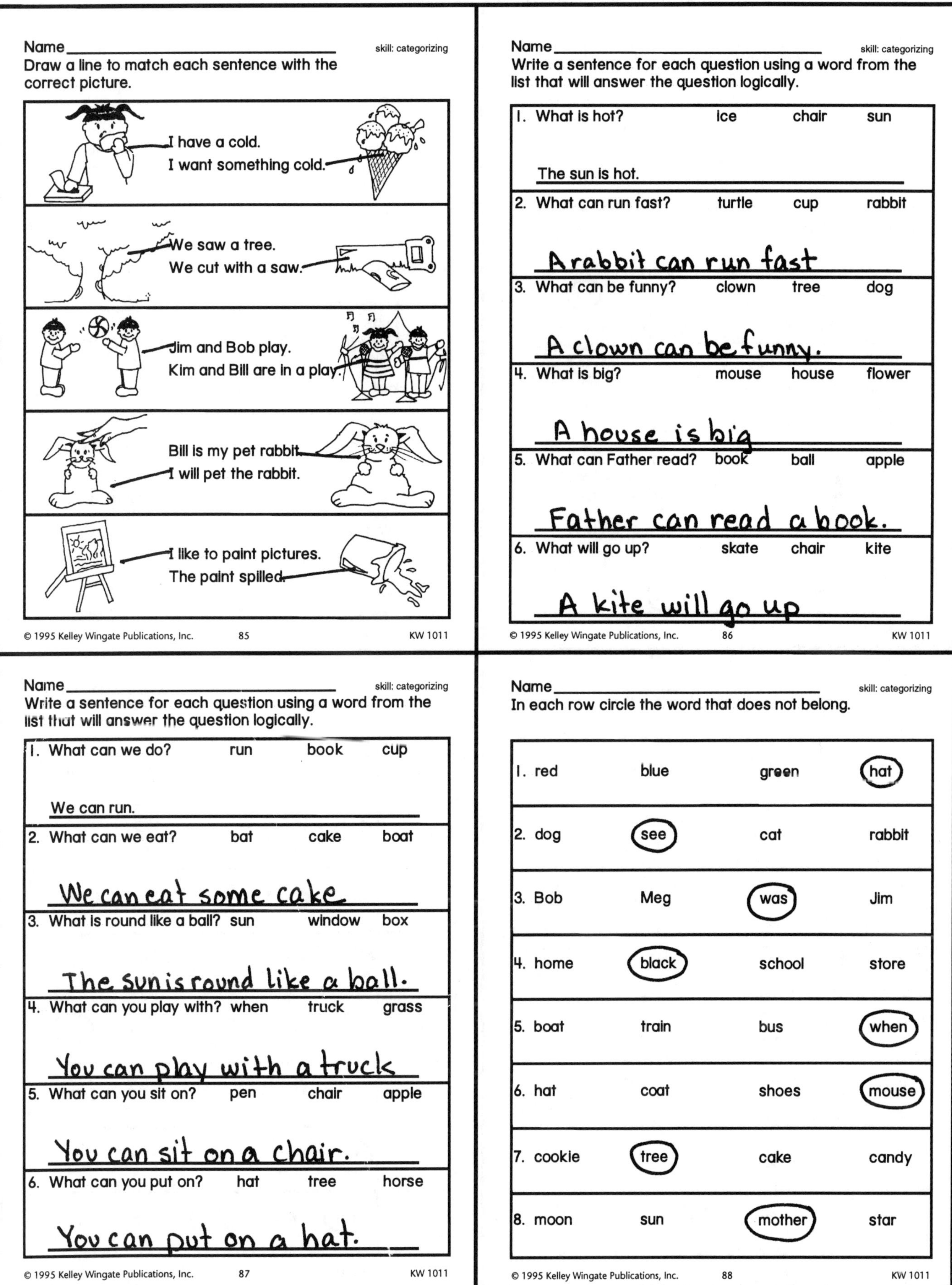

Name
skill: categorizing
Draw a line to match each sentence with the correct picture.
I have a cold.
I want something cold.
We saw a tree.
We cut with a saw.
Jim and Bob play.
Kim and Bill are in a play.
Bill is my pet rabbit.
I will pet the rabbit.
I like to paint pictures.
The paint spilled.
© 1995 Kelley Wingate Publications, Inc. 85 KW 1011
Name
skill: categorizing
Write a sentence for each question using a word from the list that will answer the question logically.
1. What is hot? ice chair sun
The sun is hot.
2. What can run fast? turtle cup rabbit
A rabbit can run fast
3. What can be funny? clown tree dog
A clown can be funny.
4. What is big? mouse house flower
A house is big
5. What can Father read? book ball apple
Father can read a book.
6. What will go up? skate chair kite
A kite will go up
© 1995 Kelley Wingate Publications, Inc. 86 KW 1011
Name
skill: categorizing
Write a sentence for each question using a word from the list that will answer the question logically.
1. What can we do? run book cup
We can run.
2. What can we eat? bat cake boat
We can eat some cake
3. What is round like a ball? sun window box
The sun is round like a ball.
4. What can you play with? when truck grass
You can play with a truck
5. What can you sit on? pen chair apple
You can sit on a chair.
6. What can you put on? hat tree horse
You can put on a hat.
© 1995 Kelley Wingate Publications, Inc. 87 KW 1011
Name
skill: categorizing
In each row circle the word that does not belong.
1. red blue green hat
2. dog see cat rabbit
3. Bob Meg was Jim
4. home black school store
5. boat train bus when
6. hat coat shoes mouse
7. cookie tree cake candy
8. moon sun mother star
© 1995 Kelley Wingate Publications, Inc. 88 KW 1011

Answer Key

Name________________________ skill: categorizing

In each row read each sentence and decide whether or not it is possible. Circle yes or no.

Yes   No

A box can jump.

Children like to play.	**Yes**	No
A fish can fly.	Yes	**No**
A tree can read.	Yes	**No**
Cake is good to eat.	**Yes**	No
All cats are black.	Yes	**No**
Ice cream is hot.	Yes	**No**
Boys and girls go to school.	**Yes**	No
A book can see.	Yes	**No**
A rabbit can hop.	**Yes**	No
Fish can laugh.	Yes	**No**
Houses can run.	Yes	**No**
You can ride on a bus.	**Yes**	No

Name________________________ skill: categorizing

What am I?

I am tall. I am green. I have a trunk. What am I? duck house **tree** man	I am small. I have words. You can read me. What am I? bike **book** bag cat
I am round. I can roll. Children play with me. What am I? doll book hat **ball**	I am yellow. I am hot I am in the sky. What am I? **sun** rain feet snow
I am round. I am silver. I can buy things. What am I? tree ball **coin** candy	I can hop. I have long ears. I am soft. What am I? cat cow cake **rabbit**

Name________________________ skill: categorizing

In each row circle the words that rhyme with the first word.

1. stop	go	**hop**	**mop**	ship	**shop**
2. play	**way**	run	**may**	**day**	ask
3. see	**three**	one	**tree**	not	**me**
4. make	**cake**	**bake**	some	have	**lake**
5. so	fish	**no**	party	**go**	ball
6. then	**pen**	saw	they	**hen**	**men**
7. look	like	**took**	**book**	**hook**	moon
8. sat	**mat**	on	**fat**	sit	**cat**

Name________________________ skill: categorizing

In each row circle the words that rhyme with the first word.

1. all	**fall**	fill	**ball**	**tall**	am
2. pat	**mat**	**sat**	can	**bat**	pull
3. will	want	**Bill**	**hill**	hall	**fill**
4. car	**bar**	**star**	can	**far**	look
5. man	**can**	and	**fan**	now	**pan**
6. dog	happy	**fog**	hand	**frog**	**log**
7. sad	**mad**	**glad**	up	silly	**dad**
8. fish	**wish**	fun	**dish**	stop	me

Answer Key

Name ______________________________ skill: context

In each row circle the word that is almost the same as the underlined word.

1. Bill is a bunny.	bear	**rabbit**	funny
2. Father is a man.	Mother	Aunt	**Dad**
3. I live on this road.	**street**	run	car
4. I was mad when I was lost.	girl	**angry**	sad
5. The elephant is big.	**large**	pig	tree
6. The mouse is small.	shoe	sky	**tiny**
7. I have a pet dog.	cat	**puppy**	log
8. I live in this house.	**home**	mouse	key

Name ______________________________ skill: context

In each row circle the word that is almost the same as the underlined word.

1. Please have a seat.	**chair**	sand	hat
2. I can run fast.	slow	fan	**quick**
3. My mother loves me.	father	**mom**	pet
4. My hat is on my head.	hot	**cap**	shoe
5. The water is cool!	**cold**	pool	can
6. A clown is happy.	old	silly	**glad**
7. Turn on the lamp.	**light**	bed	sun
8. We will leave now.	see	**go**	like

Name ______________________________ skill: context

In each row fill in the blank with the correct word to complete the sentence.

1. Meg_______a party.	**had**	have
2. It_______a good party.	**was**	were
3. Bob and Jim_______.	come	**came**
4. Peg was_______, too.	**there**	then
5. They_______many games.	play	**played**
6. Peg said, "_______is a good party".	The	**This**
7. Meg will_______the cake.	**get**	got
8. She_______eveyone a piece.	give	**gives**
9. The cake_______good.	**is**	am
10. We all_______a good time.	has	**had**

Name ______________________________ skill: context

In each row fill in the blank with the correct word to complete the sentence.

1. Meg and Peg_______playing.	**are**	was
2. They_______a ball and a rope.	**have**	has
3. Bob and Jim_______to play, too.	**want**	when
4. They want to _______ games.	**play**	played
5. They can play a fun_______.	**game**	games
6. They will all_______fast.	**run**	ran
7. Bob can run_______than Jim.	fast	**faster**
8. He may_______ the race.	**win**	wins
9. Bob_______running too soon.	stop	**stops**
10. Jim _______the winner.	**is**	are

Answer Key

Name____________________ skill: context

Read the story and answer the questions.

Toad

Bob found an animal. He thought it was a frog. He knew that a frog is green. This animal was brown. A frog is smooth. This animal was bumpy. Bob's animal was really a toad!

1. What did Bob think he found?
   a frog
2. What color was the animal?
   brown
3. Is a frog brown?
   no
4. Was the animal bumpy or smooth?
   bumpy
5. Is a frog bumpy or smooth?
   smooth
6. What was Bob's animal?
   a toad

 97 KW 1011

Name____________________ skill: context

Read the story and answer the questions.

The Rainbow

It was raining. It had rained all day. Meg wanted to take a walk. She put on her yellow raincoat. She put on her yellow boots. She opened the door and went outside. The rain had stopped and the sun was out. There was a rainbow in the sky.

1. How long had it been raining?
   all day
2. What did Meg want to do?
   take a walk
3. What two things did Meg put on?
   raincoat, boots
4. Why did Meg wear boots?
   to keep her feet dry.
5. What happened when Meg went outside?
   the rain stopped
6. Where was the rainbow?
   in the sky

 98 KW 1011

Name____________________ skill: context

Read the story and answer the questions.

The Library

Bob and Meg like to go to the library. There are many books at the library. Bob looks at books about stars and planets. Meg looks at a book about pets. They each pick two books to borrow. They can take the books home for two weeks. Then they must bring the books back.

1. Where did Meg and Bob go?
   to the library
2. What kind of books did Bob look at?
   books about stars and planets
3. Meg looked at a book. What was it about?
   pets
4. What is a library?
   a place where books are
5. How many books did they each pick?
   two
6. Can Meg and Bob keep the books?
   no
7. Name something you can borrow.
   ____

 99 KW 1011

Name____________________ skill: context

Read the story and answer the questions.

Camping

Jim and Bob wanted to go camping, but they had no tent. They had an idea. Jim tied a rope between two trees. Bob put an old blanket over the rope. The boys opened the blanket and put heavy rocks on the four corners. They were ready to camp in the backyard.

1. What did the boys want to do?
   go camping
2. What did they need?
   a tent
3. Where did they make the tent?
   in the backyard
4. Why did they need heavy rocks?
   to hold the blanket down.
5. What four things did they use to make the tents?
   rope, blankets, rocks, trees
6. Why did they need a tent to go camping?
   to have a place to sleep.

 100 KW 1011

Super Reader Award

____

receives this award for

____

Keep up the great work!

______________________ ______________

signed date

Reading Award

____

receives this award for

____

Great Job!

______________________ ______________

signed date

Great Job!

____

Receives this award for

____

Keep up the great work!

____________________ ____________________

Signed Date

Great Job!

____

Receives this award for

____

Keep up the great work!

______________ Signed

______________ Date

Congratulations!

____

Receives this award for

____

Keep up the great work!

______________ Signed

______________ Date

a	across	all	am
and	animals	are	at
baby	back	ball	balloons
because	behind	big	bike

black	blew	blue	book
boy	broken	brown	bus
cake	came	can	cat
children	circus	class	color

comes	cookie	cow	day
down	eat	farm	fast
father	fed	feet	fell
fish	friend	funny	games

gave	girl	good	green
had	has	he	helped
her	hid	home	horse
is	it	jumped	laugh

like	lions	little	make
many	milk	most	mother
most	much	name	now
old	party	pet	play

race	read	sister	skates
stop	story	table	tall
there	this	they	took
toys	wagon	yard	yellow